GARDENING BY DESIGN

WARD·LOCK

THE WATER GARDEN

PHILIP SWINDELLS

D1456207

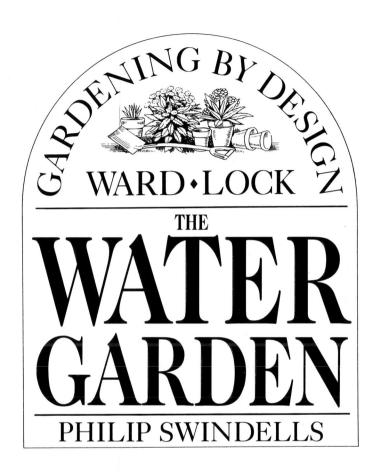

GARDENING BY DESIGN

WARD · LOCK

THE WATER GARDEN

PHILIP SWINDELLS

WARD LOCK

© Ward Lock Ltd 1985

Original edition first published as
Ward Lock Book of the Water Garden

This edition first published in Great Britain in 1990
by Ward Lock Limited, Villiers House,
41-47 Strand, London WC2N 5JE, a Cassell company.

Reprinted 1991

All Rights Reserved. No part of this publication
may be reproduced, stored in a retrieval system,
or transmitted, in any form or by any means,
electronic, mechanical, photocopying, recording,
or otherwise, without the prior permission of the
Copyright owners.

House editor Denis Ingram

Text set in Goudy Old Style
by Advance Filmsetters (Glasgow) Ltd

Printed and bound in Spain by
Graficas Reunidas

British Library Cataloguing in Publication Data
Swindells, Philip
    The water garden. – 2nd
    1. Water gardens
    I. Title   II. Swindells, Philip
    635.9'674

ISBN 0-7063 6897-5

Cover photograph
The pickerel, *Pontaderia cordata*, courtesy Harry
Smith Horticultural Photographic Collection.

Frontispiece: A picturesque cottage pool, courtesy
Mrs A. M. Sitwell (owner) and David Glover
(photographer).

Contents

Acknowledgements

The publishers gratefully acknowledge the following persons, agencies and company for granting permission for reproduction of the colour photographs: Harold Langford (pp. 10, 15, 42, 51 & 66); Harry Smith Horticultural Photographic Collection (pp. 11, 14, 59, 62, 67 & 71); Derek Gould (pp. 18, 27, 30, 31, 34 & 39); Stapeley Water Gardens Ltd. (pp. 19, 22, 23 & 26); David Glover (p. 38); and the Florapic Library (pp. 43, 46, 47, 50, 54, 55, 58, 63 & 70).

All line drawings are by Stewart Perry.

The drawings on pp. 21 & 56 are after the drawings on pp. 14 & 21 respectively in *Making the most of Water Gardening*, Philip Swindells, Floraprint, 1981. The drawings on pp. 25, 28, 29, 33, 40, 44, 48 & 49 (Fig. 10) are after illustrations appearing in the Stapeley Water Gardens Catalogue 1983. The drawings on p. 57 are after Fig. 11 in *The Water Gardening Handbook*, Philip Swindells, Croom Helm, 1984.

1 INTRODUCTION

Water gardening is a relatively new activity for the home gardener. While water certainly found a place in the past in the landscapes of famous gardeners like Capability Brown, this was scarcely water gardening as we know it today. The old masters merely dammed streams and created lakes to break up the landscape or else reflect its beauty. Only during the last 100 years has the active cultivation of aquatic plants for decoration been practised, and then widely only during the last 25 years. The cause of this revolution has been the introduction of the pool-liner and the preformed pool which have taken much of the heartache and hard work out of pool construction. Also, more is understood nowadays about the balance of life within a pool, so the much-quoted passage of the father of English gardening, William Robinson, in his classic *The English Flower Garden* (1895) scarcely applies now: 'Unclean and ugly pools deface our gardens; some have a mania for artificial water, the effect of water pleasing them so well that they bring it near their houses where they cannot have its good effects. But they have instead the filth that gathers in stagnant water and its evil smell on many a lawn.'

Water in the garden has a peculiar fascination which is shared by young and old alike, whether it be tumbling over rocks and splashing into a pool alive with the reds and yellows of goldfish, or in some sheltered nook supporting the broad verdant pads and brightly coloured waxy blossoms of the water lilies. However, it is the *position* in which such a feature is placed that will decide more than any other single factor whether this ideal can be translated into reality.

Apart from the aesthetic considerations, those governing the welfare of plants and livestock must be taken into account if a healthy balance is to be subsequently maintained. All aquatic plants enjoy full uninterrupted sunlight and, although some will tolerate shade, these are usually the more sombre and less sophisticated subjects which the average gardener in the confines of a small artificial pool cannot spare the room to grow anyway. Fish likewise require as much sunlight as possible if they are to retain their brilliant colours and make satisfactory growth, although they do appreciate a shady corner in which to glide during the heat of a summer's day. But it follows that if a pool is placed in full sun, strong plant growth will result, which will in turn ensure that there is always plenty of surface shade available for the fish.

With a natural pool it is impossible to select its position or shape and it is foolish to attempt to convert such a natural asset into an artificial formal pool. Nature's ingenuity in placing such a feature in a natural setting is such that it can be only marginally improved upon, and then only by skilful planting rather than major structural alterations.

Practical considerations aside, the visual aspect must be carefully accommodated, for, even with a small area of water, the position in which it is placed can make or mar the garden. Time taken in combining the all-important practical requirements and aesthetic considerations is time well spent, for an ill-conceived pool constructed in the wrong part of the garden is a liability. Unlike other garden features, once sited it is difficult to move.

Siting the pool

Visually a pool should be in the lowest part of the landscape, whether that landscape be of magnificent proportions or the back garden of a suburban semi-detached house. The effect in both cases is similar. Water is ill at ease when situated higher than the surrounding ground, almost as if it is im-

[*Text continues on p. 12*

A rockery in the background enhances the tranquillity of this delightful pool. Water lilies shown are: *Nymphaea marliacea* 'Chromatella' (foreground), *Nymphaea marliacea* 'Carnea' (centre right), *Nymphaea alba* (centre left), and *Nymphaea* 'Attraction' (background left).

This photograph shows how a generous planting of bog plants (irises, background; primulas, foreground) softens the hard outline of a small pool and allows it to blend easily with the rest of the garden.

patient to tumble to a lower area. Only when restricted by the sharp lines of formality does it seem at rest. Then it can be confined to a raised pool without offending the eye.

Obviously in the average garden it may be impossible or undesirable to place the pool in the lower part. Perhaps it would be overhung by trees or shaded by nearby buildings. In such circumstances the pool should be placed in a more amenable situation and, by the careful dispersal of excavated soil, made to appear that it is in fact lower than it really is. This may sound difficult to achieve, but if surplus soil is used to lift the area behind the pool, or a rock garden is constructed to the rear, then the illusion is remarkably simple to contrive.

Protection from the prevailing wind can often be provided by rock outcrops or carefully planted shrubs in the background. Protection from the wind is not only useful during the winter, but also during the early spring when young plant growth is emerging. Later in the season, when aquatic plants are approaching maturity, wind protection will be invaluable in preventing the taller marginal subjects from toppling into the pool.

Protective planting can also create problems. During autumn, leaves of nearby deciduous shrubs will accumulate in the water unless the surface of the pool is protected with netting. This precaution should in any event be taken, for decaying vegetation in the water generates toxic gases which can be lethal for fish, particularly during winter when the pool becomes covered with ice and these gases have no means of escaping into the air. Some leaves are especially toxic: those of evergreens like holly and laurel, as well as horse chestnut and willows. The seeds of the beautiful spring-flowering laburnum are particularly toxic, for they contain a soluble alkaloid which will very quickly spell the demise of the fish.

Weeping trees are often associated with water, but from the foregoing one can appreciate that they are not generally suited to poolside planting. Apart from the obvious problems that they cause, certain species, like flowering cherries and plums, are the overwintering hosts of the troublesome water lily aphid, a menace that is as devastating to succulent aquatic plants as the black bean aphid is to broad beans. Weeping willow roots undermine the foundations of con-crete pools and their leaves pollute the water with a toxic chemical akin to aspirin. Trees of a pendulous habit are for streams and riversides where their fallen leaves can be whisked away by the rains of autumn and winter.

A final consideration when deciding upon the location of the pool is the proximity of an electrical supply, for, if a fountain or waterfall is contemplated, this should be fairly close at hand.

Formality and informality

While the position which a pool occupies in the garden is vital from both a practical and visual point of view, the design which the pool-owner adopts should not be neglected. Structurally sound pools in ideal situations are often spoiled by a lack of imagination in tying them in with their surroundings. While many gardens combine formality and informality satisfactorily in adjacent areas, and often to a limited extent within the same part of the garden, a pool must strictly adhere to the overall aspect of its surroundings. Formal beds and borders must be accompanied by a formal pool, while a cottage garden atmosphere dictates an informal feature.

A formal pool often serves a different function from an informal one, for in an appropriate setting it is often used to mirror the garden around it. Thus its surface may only occasionally be punctuated by groups of water lilies and its edges graced with a restrained selection of marginal plants carefully placed so as to balance the visual aspect of the pool and yet not spoil its reflective qualities. Formality has little bearing upon the materials that the pool is constructed from. Prefabricated fibreglass pools, pool-liners and traditional concrete can all yield a first-class formal water feature, for this aspect of the design merely affects the surface, the shape that the pool takes and, to a lesser extent, the manner in which it adjoins the surrounding garden. Thus paving and walling can be used to effect in such a situation, while these materials scarcely have a use around the edge of an informal pool.

A formal pool should be a square, rectangle, circle, oval, or a combination of such symmetrical shapes, each counterbalanced so that the overall visual effect is one of equilibrium. The same applies to waterfalls or fountain features and, as intimated earlier, in certain cases with the planting too. However, that is not to say that the appearance of the pool should take precedence over the well-being of its inhabitants, for, as will be seen later, the correct ratio of plant types is necessary to ensure the sparkling clear water which all pool-owners desire. So in some cases a compromise must be made, although this should not substantially alter the overall effect of formality.

Informality in the water garden is more difficult to achieve and maintain satisfactorily. With a formal pool the gardener knows exactly where he is and can ruthlessly cull any plants that step out of line. This is not so easy to practise in the informal pool, for part of its charm is its tangled informality. Order must be kept and, while the regimentation of plants is not to be recommended, aquatics in an informal situation must be regularly kept in check. The pool itself, while being irregular in shape, should not be cluttered with fussy niches and contortions that are difficult to construct and frustrating to maintain. The water area itself should also seem to merge with the surrounding garden. Many gardeners believe that an informal pool should be planted liberally, with water lilies obscuring areas of the water surface, and reeds and rushes tumbling into the garden. While the plantsman will enjoy growing as wide a diversity of plant material as possible, the appeal of some areas of open water should not be overlooked. In an informal setting some reflections or movement of water can be equally desirable. Observe what nature does and try to emulate it.

Natural water

Fortunate indeed is the gardener blessed with a natural pond. He has a great advantage, for seldom need anything be done to alter its physical features: it is merely a question of dressing it with suitable plants. Often the marginal areas of a natural pool are inadequate and these may need altering, but apart from this it is prudent to leave as nature intended.

A perfect setting for a small, formal pool. Note how the herbaceous border around the perimeter of the paving both softens the edge of the paving and enhances the size of the pool.

A rock garden pool. Note how the relatively massive rocks in the background and the two different water levels encourage the illusion of a naturally occurring watercourse.

2 Constructing the Pool

One can readily appreciate that what applies to the siting and design of the pool also applies to the internal structure. Careful thought must be given to the requirements of the plants and livestock and suitable accommodation provided. Once again, time must be taken to consider all aspects of the project, for a pool once installed is a very permanent feature. Adequate provision must be made for the various kinds of aquatic plants, for some prefer the shallows around the pool while others require much deeper water. Reeds, rushes and other marginal subjects like marsh marigolds and irises prefer to occupy shallow shelves at the edge of the pool. These should be about 23 cm (9 in) deep and of similar width if they are to accommodate aquatic planting baskets properly. The depth may seem excessive for plants that enjoy the shallows, but it must be realised that the planting basket will raise the plants to within a few inches of the surface of the water. Water lilies and other deep-water aquatics grow in the deeper central portion of the pool. Usually this is at least 38 cm (15 in) deep, but benefits from being deeper, particularly if overwintering fancy goldfish outside is envisaged. Before deciding upon which pool to purchase or construct, it is as well to browse through one or two specialist aquatics suppliers' catalogues. Then one can judge what provisions need be made for the desired fish and plant life.

Modern materials have taken much of the hard work out of water gardening. No longer are puddled clay or gault pools constructed, when one used to have to line the excavation with soot to prevent earthworms from poking through the carefully laid finish. On warm days the area between lawn and water surface constantly had to be watched so that, immediately signs of shrinkage appeared, water could be sprayed on to the puddled surface. Fortunately, those days are over, but it would be deceitful to suggest that constructing a pool was anything other than hard work, for even with modern materials a considerable amount of energy has to be expended. What modern materials have done is create options over construction, and ease maintenance after installation.

The concrete pool

The concrete pool still has its adherents and rightly so, for a properly laid concrete pool is as good as any other and has the added advantage of being flexible in design. This design should embody all the aspects discussed, but is often difficult for the newcomer to visualise. So, before lifting the spade, take a length of rope or hosepipe and mark out the pool's shape on the ground. This ensures that the pool fits into the general scene and is of compatible size. The external shape can then be marked out with the spade and the excavation begun. This marking-out to get an impression of the finished feature is not peculiar to concrete pools, for it will be realised that any pool made with a material that the gardener can mould to suit his whim can be assessed this way before excavations begin.

With a concrete pool it has to be appreciated at the outset that the excavation is going to be considerably larger than the finished pool, for room must be allowed for the layer of concrete. Indeed, the excavation should be at least 15 cm (6 in) larger than the finished pool to allow for a generous layer of concrete, and the soil should be rammed down tightly to prevent any subsidence and ensure a firm base. A layer of heavy-gauge builders' polythene can then be used to line the excavation as a safety precaution against leaking, but also as a means of retaining moisture within the setting concrete so that it dries as slowly as possible. Newly laid concrete that dries quickly often develops hair cracks which

[Text continues on p. 20

Fig. 1. Construction of a concrete pool.

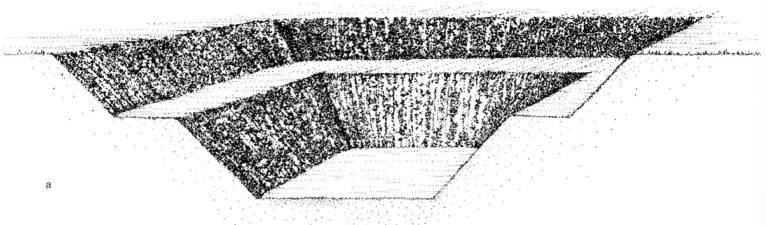

a

(*a*) The soil is excavated to the required shape. In this case it has been decided to have a marginal shelf running around the pool about 23 cm (9 in) below the surface – hence the stepped design. When excavating, remember to allow for the space taken by the concrete – at least 15 cm (6 in) all the way round.

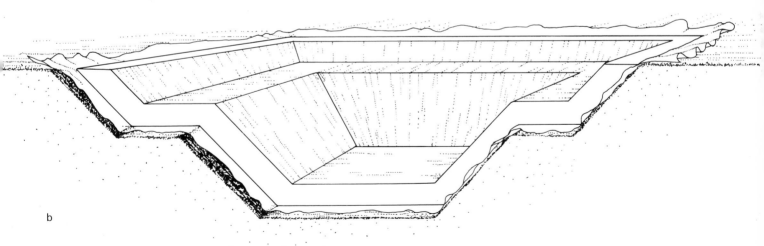

b

(*b*) Having rammed the soil down firmly to ensure a firm base, a layer of heavy-gauge builder's polythene is used to line the excavation as a safety precaution against leaking and also to help retain moisture within the setting concrete so that it dries as slowly as possible. The concrete is laid to a depth of 10 cm (4 in) over the floor and up the sides. If the sides are very steep, it may be necessary to erect some formwork to hold the concrete while it is setting.

[*Fig. 1 continues on p. 21*

17

Opposite: The soft curves of this informal pool are particularly pleasing to the eye. In the centre of the pool is the water hawthorn (*Aponogeton distachyus*) and in right background golden club (*Orontium aquaticum*).

Above: A simple, kidney-shaped pool, the construction of which is easily within the scope of the amateur DIY householder (see pp. 24–32). Note how the irises form a good backdrop for the water lilies.

then become potential points of weakness in the surface.

It is ideal if concreting can be carried out during one day as there is then less likelihood of a leak appearing. When this proves to be impossible, the edge of the previous day's work should be roughed up so that the new mix will key with it. Under no circumstances should the time that elapses between mixes extend beyond 24 hours, or leaks are almost inevitable. I prefer to get the concrete in already mixed. It does present some problems, as once ordered the concrete will come irrespective of the weather. Notwithstanding that, ready-mixed concrete does have the great advantage of being consistently mixed, can have a waterproofing compound added to it before you get it, and saves the mixing time (which can mean the difference between the pool being completed in a single day and taking two or three). However, some people like to mix their own concrete; others do so on financial grounds, while a few feel that the lorry cannot get close enough to the site to make the upheaval that it inevitably causes worthwhile.

While mixing concrete is hard physical work, there is nothing terribly complicated or mystical about it. A good mixture consists of 1 part cement, 2 parts sand and 4 parts 2 cm ($\frac{3}{4}$ in) gravel measured out with a shovel or bucket. Mix a sufficient quantity to make the effort worthwhile, but do not be tempted to mix a vast quantity each time as it will be difficult to get the mix of even consistency. It is turned over and mixed in its dry state until of a uniform greyish colour. If a waterproofing compound is to be added, it is done at this stage. Water is then added and mixing continued until the agglomeration is of a wet, yet stiff, consistency. A useful guide as to its readiness is to place a shovel into the mixture, withdrawing it in a series of jerks so that the ridges that are formed retain their character. If they collapse immediately, then they are either too wet or too dry and the mixture must be amended before use. Some pool-owners prefer their concrete pool to have a coloured finish and this can be provided during the mixing stage. Pigments mixed in with the cement at the dry mix stage, in quantities up to 10% by weight, give a good even colouring. Chromium oxide gives a green finish, red iron oxide a tawny red, cobalt blue a blue, and manganese black a black, while the use of Snowcrete cement and fine Derbyshire spar ensures a first-class white surface.

When the concrete is ready, it should be laid to a depth of 10 cm (4 in) over the floor of the pool and up the sides as well. If the pool sides are vertical or very steep, it may be necessary to erect some kind of formwork. Rough planks can be used in a formal pool with square or rectangular sides, but marine plywood and a series of props and strengtheners are necessary when an irregular shape has to be catered for. To reduce the risk of the concrete sticking to the formwork, it is advisable to grease or limewash it, although in practice a thorough soaking with clean water will have the desired effect. Once a layer covers the entire pool shape, a reinforcing layer of 5 cm (2 in) mesh chicken-wire netting is placed over the wet concrete. A final 5 cm (2 in) layer of concrete is then added and given a smooth finish with a plasterer's trowel.

An hour or two after completion, when any lingering surface water has disappeared, all the exposed areas of the concrete should be covered with wet hessian sacks to prevent the concrete drying out too quickly. In hot summer weather this frequently happens and, when drying is rapid, hair cracks appear. If the area to be covered is too large to contemplate with damp sacks, then the regular spraying of the surface of the concrete with clean water, from a watering can fitted with a fine rose attachment, will have the desired effect. It depends upon the weather, but after a week or so the concrete will have dried sufficiently to be treated prior to the introduction of fish and plants.

Concrete contains a considerable amount of free lime which is harmful in varying degrees to both fish and plants. This dissipates with weathering, so, if your pool is constructed during late summer and is likely to remain empty throughout the winter, it will 'cure' itself. The same effect can be obtained by filling the pool with water and emptying it several times over a period of two or three weeks. At the same time it is recommended that sufficient potassium permanganate crystals be added to the water to turn it violet. What this latter achieves I am not quite sure, but I have yet to hear of a gardener who has experienced any problems with free lime after following this recommendation. However, the simplest method to overcome this potential problem is to fill the pool once with clear water and allow it to stand for about a week. Then empty it and allow it to dry.

[Text continues on p. 24

Fig. 1. Construction of a concrete pool – *continued*

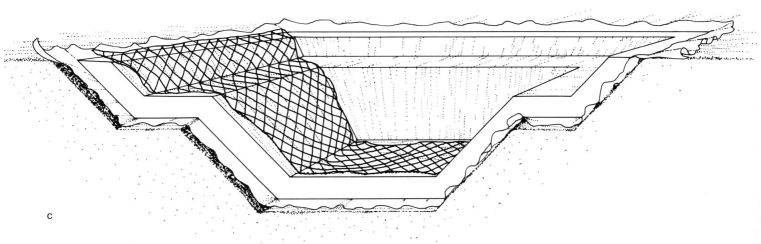

c

(c) When the entire pool shape has been covered with its first layer of concrete, a reinforcing layer of 5 cm (2 in) mesh chicken wire is placed over the still wet concrete.

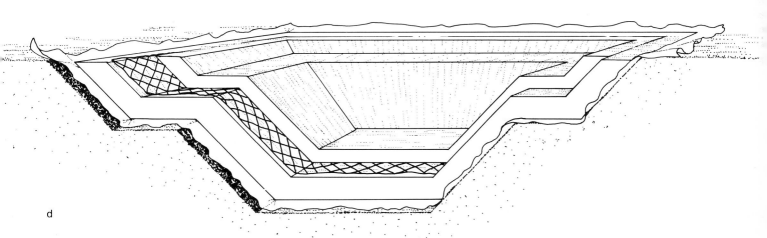

d

(d) A final 5 cm (2 in) layer of concrete is then added and given a smooth finish with a plasterer's trowel. After an hour or two of completion, cover all the exposed surfaces with wet hessian sacks to prevent the concrete drying out too quickly, a hazard which can easily occur in the hot summer months.

A larger pool than that shown on p. 19, this one is more ambitious in that it incorporates a waterfall. Plants include waterlilies, flowering rush (left foreground), irises, greater spearwort (*Ranunculus lingua* 'Grandiflora') left midground, and *Scirpus tabernaemontani* right background.

Even more ambitious than the one opposite, this pool has both a waterfall and fountain. Note that the stepped rockery provides a more interesting background than would a completely flat area.

The surface can then be treated with a neutralizing agent like the universally known Silglaze. This is available as a white powder which is mixed with water and painted on to the concrete. Not only does it neutralize the free lime, but also seals the pool by internal glazing. Rubber-based and liquid plastic paints also prevent free lime from escaping when painted over the entire surface of the concrete. In most cases it is important to use a special primer first, or else the paint will flake and peel away, following a chemical reaction between it and the raw concrete. These paints are available in a number of natural and unnatural colours and, while giving the pool a good waterproof finish, are rather expensive to contemplate for large expanses.

Pool-liners

Pool-liners are a popular form of construction, and justifiably so, for they are available in a range of sizes and materials that are within the reach of all but the most impecunious. The pool constructed from a liner can be as large and irregular as the gardener fancies and yet can be adapted simply to accommodate a bog garden as well. Most popular pool-liners consist merely of a sheet of heavy-gauge polythene or rubber material which is placed in the excavation and moulded to its contours. The water holds it in place within the pool while it is secured at the top by rocks, paving slabs or turf. Selecting the most suitable kind of pool-liner can be rather confusing; prices vary widely for products that, to the uninitiated, appear to be very similar.

The popular end of the market and consequently the cheapest pool-liners are those made from 500 gauge polythene in a light blue colour and made in various standard sizes. These usually make quite a small pool and can frequently be purchased from department stores as well as from garden centres and water-gardening specialists. However, they cannot be unreservedly recommended to the gardener who requires something fairly permanent. While it is quite true that, with exceptional care, a polythene liner is capable of lasting for 10 years or more, it is more likely that it will perish within three, the area between the water surface and ground level being bleached by the sun, cracking and falling away. In most circumstances the polythene liner has little to recommend it except as a cheap temporary home for fish and plants while the main pool is being cleaned out.

The pool-liners which fall into the next category are what one might call in the medium-price range and represent good value for the average newcomer to water gardening. They are usually of a polyvinylchloride (PVC) material and available in pastel shades as well as imitation pebble. While most are manufactured in handy sizes to make popular-sized pools, it is quite possible, for a little extra expense, to have one made to personal specifications. Likewise, in the more expensive rubber class, liners are often prepacked, but specific orders can be prepared too. The rubber liners are of the same material as used by farmers for irrigation lagoons and by local authorities for sailing and boating lakes. They have a black matt finish and are exceptionally durable, although some of the PVC ones, with their reinforcing welded Terylene web, are fairly comparable.

Choosing the liner is one thing, calculating the size is quite another, for it always appears that you require a vast sheet for even quite a modest pool. The reason for this is that you do not just calculate the length and breadth of the pool, but the various areas that are going to accommodate marginal shelves as well. Sufficient surplus should be left at the top to allow an anchorage with stones or paving slabs and, when an irregular-shaped pool is envisaged, then calculations should be based upon a rectangle which encloses the greatest width and breadth of the excavation.

All liners are installed in a broadly similar manner, those made from polythene being spread out on the lawn in the sun for an hour or two before installation in order to become more supple and mould to the excavation more readily. The hole should be scoured for any sharp objects likely to puncture the liner, for it should be remembered that, once water is added, the pressure of the liner against the walls and floor of the pool, and consequently against any sharp stone or twig, is such that it can be ultimately forced through the liner. To prevent this happening, it is useful to spread a layer of sand over the floor of the pool and along the marginal shelves to act as a cushion. A similar effect can be

[Text continues on p. 32

Fig. 2. Construction of pool with a liner.

a

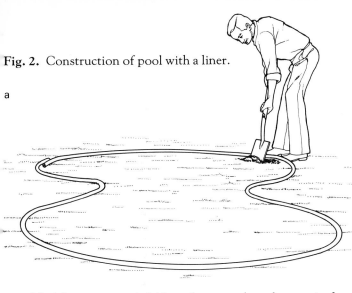

(a) A hose or rope is laid on the ground, to the required shape and size of the proposed pool. Commence digging, always cutting the turf or soil on the *inside* of the hose/rope, as shown here.

b

(b) Proceed with the excavation, leaving marginal shelves as required 23 cm (9 in) wide and 23 cm (9 in) below water level. The pool perimeter is also cut back sufficiently to allow for the pool edging.

c

(c) Short wooden pegs are inserted 90–120 cm (3–4 ft) apart around the pool and the tops levelled using a spirit level. It is important that the top edge of the pool be levelled as, on filling the pool, the water level will immediately show any non-levelness in the edging surface.

d

(d) After the final shaping has been completed, the width and depth of the marginal shelves should be checked. The sides and floor of the excavation should also be checked for the presence of any sharp stones or roots which, if found, should be removed.

[*Fig. 2 continues on p. 28*]

Above: This unusually-sited pool beside a sloping driveway provides immediate impact at the entrance of this property. The plants beside the pool at the rear help it to merge with the surrounding landscape.

Opposite: A large, kidney-shaped pool at Brobury House, near Hay-on-Wye, Herefordshire, with an ornamental statue providing a focus of interest.

Fig. 2. Construction of a pool with a liner – *continued*

e

f

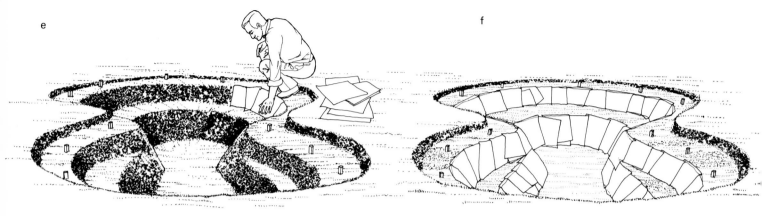

(e) A cushion of sand 1·2 cm (½ in) deep should be placed on the floor of the excavation and on the horizontal surfaces of the marginal shelves. A layer of wet newspapers is used to cushion the sloping sides.

(f) The finished excavation should be as neat and trim as possible – any irregularity in the surface will show after the liner has been fitted. The level pegs should be removed before the liner is laid.

g

h

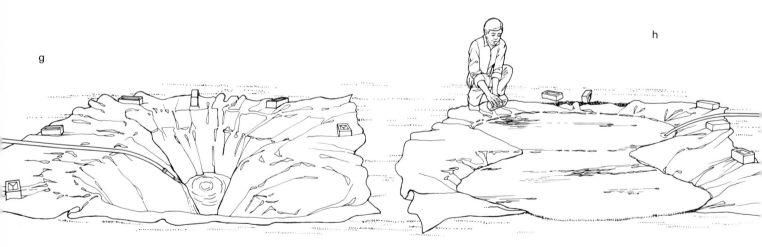

(g) The pool liner is draped loosely into the excavation with as even an overlap as possible all round. Bricks or stones are placed on the overlap and water filling is then started by means of a hose.

(h) As the pool fills, the stones should be eased off at intervals to allow the liner to fit snugly into the contours of the excavation. Some creasing is inevitable but it can be minimized by judicious stretching as the pool fills.

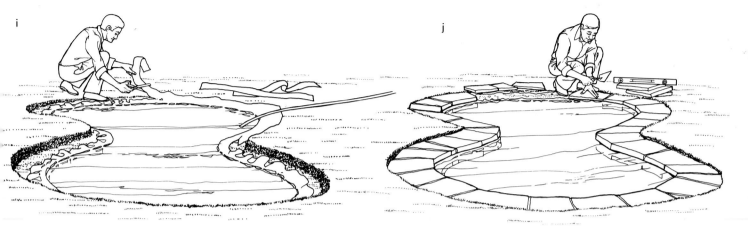

(i) When the pool is full, the surplus lining is cut off leaving a 10–13 cm (4–5 in) flap. To ensure the liner does not slip, weight it down with stones.

(j) The pool is then edged either with broken slats or, better, natural paving. The paving is laid on a bed of mortar 3 parts sand to 1 part cement.

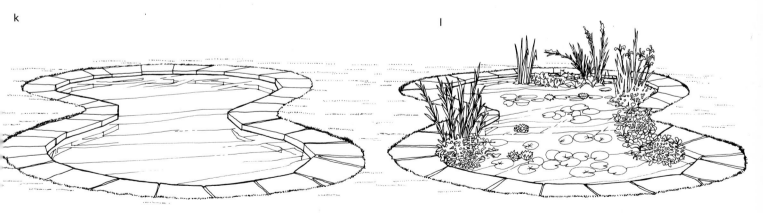

(k) The finished pool. If cement has dropped into the water during construction work, the pool must be emptied and re-filled before planting and stocking with fish.

(l) The pool is planted and, in time, will assume an established look. Fountains, lighting and other ornaments can now be added, if desired.

Having two pools at different levels allows for the provision of a simple, yet extremely tranquil waterfall, such as shown here.

A waterfall emerging from a secret grotto. The illusion that the water emanates from a natural spring is achieved by a submersible pump – please see p. 48 for details.

obtained for the walls by taking wads of newspaper and wetting them thoroughly before packing them against the walls in papier mâché style.

As polythene liners have little elasticity, they are installed without water being added, but plenty of movement should be catered for, so that, when the water is gradually introduced, the wrinkles can be smoothed out and the liner moulded to the contours of the hole. Rubber and PVC liners can be stretched across the excavation and weighted down with rocks or paving slabs. As the water is added and the liner tightens, the anchoring weights around the pool are slowly released until the pool becomes full and the liner moulds to its exact shape. Once the pool is full and as many of the unsightly wrinkles as possible have been smoothed out, superfluous material from around the edges can be trimmed, but do not neglect to allow sufficient for anchoring with stones or paving slabs. The pool is then immediately ready for planting, for pool-liners do not contain anything that is toxic to fish or aquatic plant life.

The pool liner also gives the gardener an opportunity to do what most other forms of construction are not flexible enough to allow, and that is to construct a bog garden as an integral part of the feature. All that is needed is a pool-liner that is larger in one dimension than necessary for the pool envisaged. This allows the development, at one end, of a spreading, shallow-pool arrangement a foot or so deep which can be readily converted into a bog garden. A retaining wall of loose bricks or stones separates the bog garden from the pool proper and retains the peaty mixture which is placed over a layer of gravel. This gives a moisture-retentative growing medium, but allows excessive wetness to drain from the roots of the plants. Water from the pool moistens the soil through the barrier, the soil level being a good inch above pool level.

Prefabricated pools

There are really two quite distinct categories of prefabricated pool: the fibreglass kind and those made of vacuum-formed plastic. The latter are the cheaper sort and are moulded in a tough weather-resistant plastic and have a roughish, undulating finish to simulate natural rock. While being inexpensive and readily transportable, they do have the disadvantage of flexibility which can cause problems during installation. Fibreglass pools are obviously entirely rigid and free-standing, and present no such difficulties during construction, but one must be very careful over the choice of design, for most are made by fibreglass manufacturers with little understanding of plant life and it is often the case that reeds, rushes and irises are expected to become established on a marginal shelf no more than 8 cm (3 in) wide, while the deeper areas of the pool will not have a sufficiently flat floor to place a single water lily basket.

There are many different shapes and sizes to choose from and most can be obtained in a choice of colours, so it is wise to obtain a selection of catalogues from specialists and weigh up the advantages and disadvantages of each type before making what will undoubtedly be a sizeable investment. As in most walks of life, you generally get what you pay for and a higher-priced product will generally be of higher quality. Read the manufacturers' descriptions carefully, for some of the smaller pools are really rock pools which are intended to sit near the summit of a rock garden so that water tumbles down a cascade unit into a pool below. These are relatively inexpensive, but are not suited to most aquatic plants nor to accommodating ornamental fish. Fountain trays are also shallow and likewise can offer little to aquatic plant life, other than possibly a few submerged oxygenating plants. These are the small pools which accommodate a fountain in a confined space or serve as a receptacle to catch water spouting from a gargoyle. Even if they are deep enough to house a few aquatic plants, it would be unwise to do this, for when used for their proper purpose, water turbulence is such that none but the coarsest and most vigorous aquatics would survive.

Having decided upon a prefabricated pool, the next stage is to get it into the ground. If you ask the retailer how you go about it, he will probably tell you to dig a hole to the desired shape and then drop it in. In theory, this sounds quite simple, but in practice it is not so. What one has to do is to dig out a rectangle that will enclose the length and breadth of

[*Text continues on p. 36*

Fig. 3. Construction of a pre-fabricated pool.

a

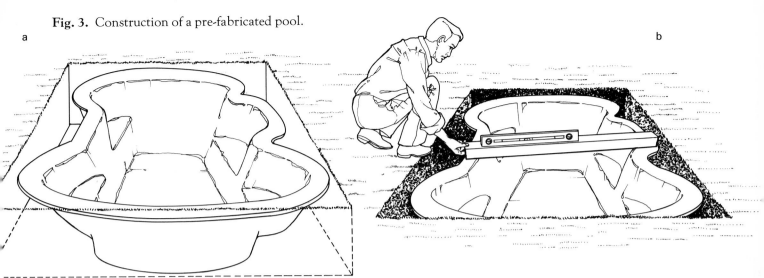

b

(*a*) Excavate a rectangular hole that will enclose the length and breadth of the pool and its greatest depth. To allow room for backfilling, make the length and breadth dimensions about 23 cm (9 in) larger than the actual dimensions of the pool. The floor should be well compacted and a 2·5 cm (1 in) layer of sand spread and levelled.

(*b*) The pool must be levelled from end to end and from side to side by means of a board and spirit level. The top edge of the pool should be an inch or so *below* the ground level, because back-filling operations will tend to raise the pool slightly.

c

d

(*c*) Commence to fill the pool and, simultaneously, to back-fill with sand or sifted soil. The water level and back-fill level should be kept the same to give maximum support to the pool. Particular care should be taken to back-fill under the shelves.

(*d*) The finished pool, edged with paving and established with marginal plants and water lilies.

Above: An exceedingly pleasant and natural looking pool in a lawn setting. Note how the pea-shingle in the scree garden and the rockery beyond enhance the naturalness of the pond's setting.

Opposite: The water garden at Clack's Farm, which was made and planted over several years, in front of BBC cameras, for 'Gardeners' World' programmes.

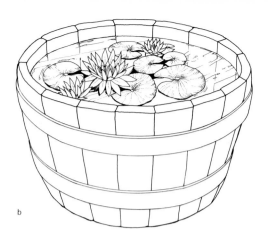

Fig. 4. Miniature water gardens.
(*a*) Sink garden. An old, glazed porcelain sink can be transformed into a water garden by coating it with an artificial stone mixture. First clean the sink. Then coat the outside with a bonding agent and, while this is still tacky, pat on a moistened mixture of 2 parts peat, 1 part sand and 1 part cement. Aim for 1·2 cm ($\frac{1}{2}$ in) thick layer all over the outside, over the lip and all the way down the inside surfaces. Leave to dry and harden for 2 weeks. When planting be careful to select plants of modest growth.

the pool and the greatest depth. The excavation will, in fact, have to be substantially larger, for it must be remembered that room must be allowed around the edge for backfilling. The pool should be placed on a generous layer of sand and the shallow end supported on bricks. It must then be levelled from end to end and side to side by means of a board and spirit level. It is important that the pool be an inch or so below the surrounding ground, for during backfilling the addition of material packed tightly behind the pool will raise it slightly. Start with the pool level with the ground and it will finish just proud, and then the edge will be difficult to disguise. The fact that the pool should be level from the outset and should be constantly checked during backfilling cannot be over-emphasized, for a pool that is out of level leads to flooding in some places and unsightly exposure of the fibreglass in others. If the soil that has been excavated is in poor physical condition, discard it and backfill with sand or pea gravel. It is important that the medium used flows and fills all the air space, to preclude subsidence later.

(*b*) Tub garden. Discarded vinegar or wine casks also make excellent small-pool containers, when sawn in half and waterproofed inside with bitumen paint. A water tub will provide two or three goldfish with a pleasant home during the summer but they should be removed for the winter.

Miniature water gardens

Any receptacle capable of holding water is a potential water garden. Old galvanized water tanks and sinks, or baths with their outlets plugged with putty are all extremely serviceable when sunk in the ground, although the former will corrode and leak unless protected initially with a good rubber-based paint. Discarded vinegar and wine casks also make excellent small pools when sawn in half, but wooden containers that have contained oil, tar or wood preservative should be avoided, as any residue that remains will pollute the water and form unsightly scum on the surface.

No matter what container you use, it is advisable to give it a thorough scrubbing with clean water. Never use detergent for cleaning, as it is difficult to be certain when all traces have been removed. In tanks or sinks where algae have become established, the addition to the water of enough potassium permanganate to turn the water a violet colour will usually have the desired effect.

Planting can be undertaken in the same way as described for the conventional pool, but be careful to select only plants that are of modest growth. Fish can spend the summer in such a container but should be removed for the winter.

3 FOUNTAINS AND WATERFALLS

Water holds a fascination for everyone, but never more so than when it is moving. With an appreciation of this, manufacturers have produced a whole range of equipment that can simulate a gentle tumbling stream, crashing waterfall or sparkling dancing fountain. Cascade or waterfall units made of fibreglass or vacuum-formed plastic are readily available in a multitude of shapes, sizes and colours. Some consist of a simple bowl with a lip, over which the water trickles, while others come in sections of varying lengths and shapes which can be joined together to form complex arrangements. Installation is simple, as the units merely need setting securely in position and the delivery hose from the pump inserted into the uppermost one before being fully operational.

A fountain can sometimes be incorporated with a waterfall by the use of a two-way junction on the pump outlet, but in most instances the pump is not sufficiently powerful to produce the desired effect. A fountain alone is a much better proposition and, by the judicious use of jets with different numbers and arrangements of holes, some pleasing spray patterns can be obtained. Apart from straightforward fountains, ornaments depicting cherubs, mermaids and similar characters can be purchased, each designed to take a pump outlet so that water can spout from their mouth, or a shell, or any similar object that they might be holding. Where space is very limited and there is insufficient room to accommodate a waterfall or fountain satisfactorily, 'masks' and gargoyles can be used with great effect. These are usually imitation lead or stone ornaments depicting the faces of gnomes, cherubs or sometimes the head of a lion, and are flat on one side to enable them to be fixed to a wall. Water is pumped up into the 'mask' and spews from the mouth into a pool below. While all these contrivances give us the pleasure of moving water, we must spare a thought for the plants beneath. Almost all aquatic plants with floating leaves dislike turbulent water or a continuous fine spray on their foliage, so any moving-water feature that is envisaged should be considered for one end of the pool and out of the direct line of choice plants like water lilies.

Choosing a pump

While it is relatively simple to establish moving water in the garden, it can be somewhat hazardous deciding upon the necessary equipment without a little background knowledge or the advice of a fellow-gardener with a similar feature. The catalogues produced by manufacturers and distributors of water pumps are so complex now that they can become difficult territory for the uninitiated, so advice should be sought from all quarters. Water-gardening specialists usually reduce the chances of making an error by offering a selection suited to the ornamental pool, so their judgement should be trusted. When it comes to installation, sound advice can be obtained from the Electricity Council, for electricity is a good servant but a poor master, and the inexperienced should not tamper with its installation, especially in the presence of water. The value of the expert's help in both departments should not be underestimated.

Submersible pumps are designed to operate completely submerged in the pool and are silent and safe to operate. As they are merely placed into the water, there is no need for a complex plumbing arrangement or a separate chamber as with surface pumps. Generally, such a pump will consist of a cast body containing a motor. An input unit attached to this will draw water into the pump, often through a filter or strainer which will catch any debris and filamentous algae likely to block the pump. The cover of this unit will be removable and the collected debris should be periodically

[Text continues on p. 41]

A cottage pond showing water lilies just at the right time
when they should be lifted and divided.

A garden pool with fountain in the grand scale, evocative
perhaps of the Broads on a summer's day.

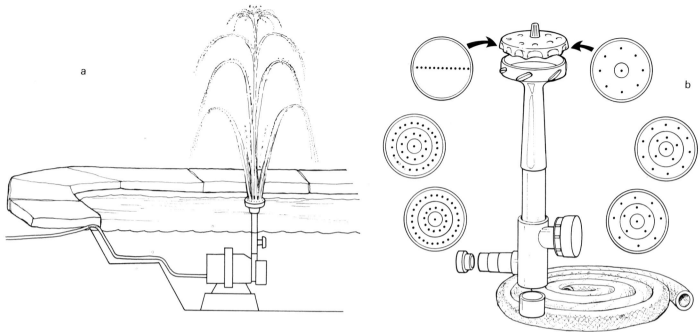

Fig. 5. Fountains.
(*a*) A sparkling fountain, achieved by means of a submersible pump, adds the interest of moving water to the pool environment. Care should be taken to site the fountain away from choice water plants such as water lilies, which dislike turbulent water or fine spray on their foliage.
(*b*) Diagram showing how several different spray patterns can be made by means of interchangeable discs at the fountain head.

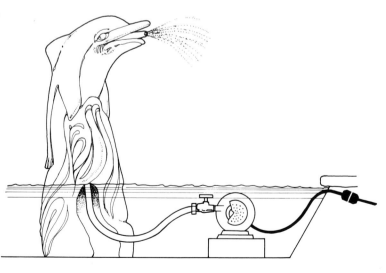

Fig. 6. Ornamental fountain.
If a more decorative fountain is required, an ornamental fountain, such as this dolphin one, can be installed. Each ornamental fountain is designed to take a pump outlet so that water can spout from its mouth, shell or similar object.

40

removed. Above the input is the adjuster assembly. This can comprise a single or double outflow to allow water to be discharged as both fountain and waterfall, although, as intimated earlier, one *or* the other is more desirable. Control can be exercised over both by the flow adjuster screw. In the case of a fountain, a jet with a series of holes in it will be attached to the outflow to create a spray pattern. Different interchangeable jets are available and these will give varying complexities and heights of spray. When a waterfall is envisaged, a length of tube sufficient to reach from the outflow to the head of the cascade is attached.

Some submersible pumps have a very small discharge and so it is important to judge the water flow required before shopping around. Most will provide an adequate fountain, but a surprising amount of water is required to operate a satisfactory waterfall. Most manufactured cascade units require an output of at least 1140 litres (250 gallons) per hour to put a thin sheet of water across their width, while 1365 litres (300 gallons) per hour is required to make a continuous filmy flow 15 cm (6 in) wide. If in doubt about the necessary

flow, an indication can be gained by using water from the tap through a hose. The output from the hose can be assessed by pouring into a container for one minute. If the amount of water collected is measured in pints and that figure multiplied by 7·5, the gallonage per hour will be calculated. It is then a relatively simple matter to assess the flow required down the watercourse.

Installation of a submersible pump is quite simple, for, as described earlier, it is merely placed in the water. It is prudent, however, to set it on a level plinth, and in the case of a fountain assembly it is vital that the jet unit be just above the maximum water level. Connection to the electricity supply should be via a weatherproof cable connector to the extension lead. The most satisfactory arrangement is to have the cable connector concealed beneath a small paving slab. This means that the pump can be easily removed from the pool without disturbing the extension cable, if maintenance proves necessary. During the winter the pump should be removed in any event, this allowing a pool-heater to be installed in its place if desired.

Fig. 7. Simple waterfall.
Sectional diagram showing how a simple waterfall can be made by means of a submersible pump, to which is attached a length of flexible tubing. Note that the pump is set on a level plinth.

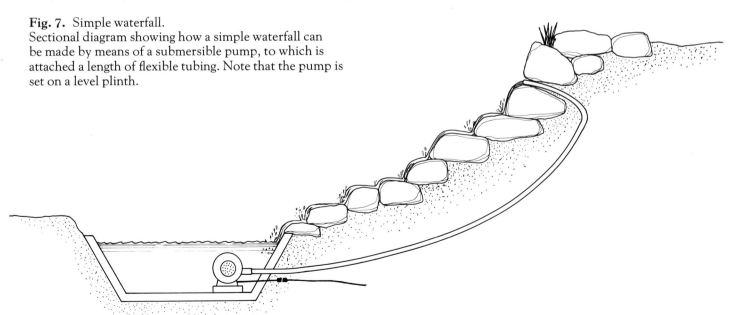

The water hyacinth (*Eichhornia crassipes*). Originating from tropical South America, this handsome plant has rosettes of leaves which grow 5–15 cm (2–6 in) in length and, in the centre of the rosettes, 15 cm (6 in) spikes of 10–30 large and showy flowers appear in summer.

Opposite: The water fringe (*Nymphoides peltata*). Native to Europe and Asia. The rounded leaves, mottled with purple, are about 5 cm (2 in) across. The plant bears large 2·5 cm (1 in) golden yellow flowers in clusters 5–7·5 cm (2–3 in) above the water. Hardy in cold climates.

Surface pumps

Surface pumps are preferable for some water gardens, especially where a relatively high 'head' of water is necessary, this 'head' being the vertical distance between water level and the highest point of discharge. If more than one fountain is desired, a surface pump is sensible and, of course, when larger volumes of water than submersible pumps can easily handle are to be moved, then they become a necessity.

The range of surface pumps available is wide, but all need to be housed in a purpose-built, well-ventilated, dry chamber. This can be either above or below the pool water level, but, when above, a foot valve and strainer must be used on the suction tube to retain the prime. When the pump is accommodated below the water level, a strainer only need be used, as the prime is maintained by gravity. However, the pump must always be housed where its vertical distance from the water level is less than the suction lift of the pump.

A surface pump consists of a cast body incorporating the motor, a suction tube with a strainer attached, and one or more delivery tubes according to the number of outlets being serviced. These tubes should be of adequate bore, without sharp bends, and as short as practicable. While the pump only has one outlet, separate delivery tubes can be attached by means of tee-pieces, but control valves are necessary to adjust the flow to each individual outlet.

Fountains

The simplest fountain is obtained by a jet unit attached to the outlet of a submersible pump, or to a figure or artificially contrived feature served by a surface pump. These are perfectly adequate for most gardeners, but the more technically appreciative and extrovert amongst us may wish to try some of the more adventurous systems currently available, especially those that incorporate varying spray patterns or coloured lighting.

The most exciting development in recent years has been the illuminated fountain. This is self-contained and provides a spectacular water display at night, yet during the daytime

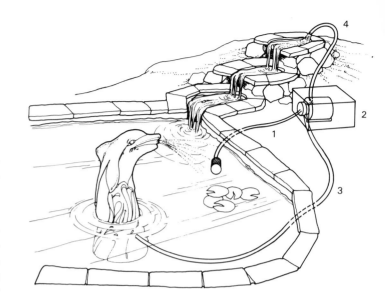

Fig. 8. Surface pump.
A surface pump must be housed in a purpose-built, well-ventilated, dry chamber. Water is sucked up the suction tube (1) into the pump (2). Delivery from the pump in this instance is divided into two tubes; one goes to the fountain in the pool (3), and the other goes to the head of the waterfall (4).

can be used as an ordinary fountain. Indeed, the addition to the conventional fountain is primarily a spotlight encased in a sealed alloy underwater lampholder unit. This is generally available with a choice of coloured lenses which give a single-colour fountain. Alternatively, manufacturers have recently produced a colour-changer. This is a revolving disc of different colour segments which automatically change the colour of the fountain. The rotation of the colour-changer can be adjusted to give slow or rapid colour change. While a conventional fountain with a standard spray pattern can be used to create a pleasing display, it has been found that, to give maximum colour density to the spray pattern, a thin columnar effect is best, and this is provided by a special jet with a larger number of fine holes. This jet can be controlled in the same way by use of the flow adjuster which is located just beneath the colour-changing unit. The pump itself is attached to the lampholder unit, which in turn is securely fastened to a specially manufactured PVC base. Another type incorporates single-colour lights immediately beneath the fountain jet, the water passing directly over and around the lamp before entering the jet.

Automatically changing spray patterns can be achieved by means of a device which can be attached to the pump. As many as 18 patterns are currently obtainable in a set sequence, with each spray pattern lasting up to 16 seconds and each complete sequence something like $3\frac{1}{2}$ minutes. It is a fitting that is suited to both submersible and surface pumps, but the more powerful the pump the higher and wider the sprays produced, with a proportionate acceleration of the time lapse between each change of spray pattern.

Fanciful spray patterns can be created with special adaptors that not only vary the height and shape of the traditional fountain, but also produce unusual water patterns. Such an innovation is the bell fountain which, by means of a single adaptor, creates a unique globular spray pattern, almost like a glass bell in appearance. Single bells are fascinating, but triple bells from a single unit are quite remarkable. Not only are they breathtakingly beautiful during the day, but they can be easily lit at night. A similar feature can be created by the use of a fountain ring. This is a tubular ring with five or more adjustable jets which can provide varying spray patterns. The ring is attached to the outflow of a submersible pump.

Adventurous fountain arrangements do not need to come readily packaged, for the ambitious gardener can create his own. One of the most imaginative that I have seen uses a series of bowls and a conventional fountain spray. Water is pumped up a tall central stem and then tumbles into a small bowl. Beneath this are bowls of the same shape and construction, but increasingly greater diameters. When the first bowl has filled, the water falls into the second and so on until it reaches the pool below. To ensure that the gently twisting curtain of water falls evenly from around each rim, it is absolutely essential that each bowl is level. The problem created by such a feature, however, is one of excessive turbulence in the pool below. To counteract this, one must consider growing few plants other than the all-important submerged oxygenating plants, or else arresting the turbulence by placing beneath the fountain a large ring which is of greater diameter than the lower bowl. Plants can then be grown in the relative peace of the perimeter.

Most fountains shoot water into the air, but a quite modest feature known as a pebble fountain is most restrained and yet very attractive. Although not technically a fountain, it utilizes the same components as the conventional fountain. In appearance it is a contained area of sizeable attractive pebbles or cobbles through which water constantly bubbles. It is easy to maintain and does not need either aquatic plant life, fish or snails. Essentially it consists of a small concrete chamber which is waterproof and can accommodate sufficient water to enable a simple submersible pump to operate. A framework of iron bars is placed across the top and this supports fine-mesh netting. On top of this a generous layer of washed pebbles or cobbles is placed and the pump outlet drawn up until it is at the surface of the stones. Water bubbles up through the pebbles, creating a cool refreshing effect. As evaporation is rapid, the chamber beneath will require regularly topping up with fresh water.

Waterfalls

Mention has already been made of waterfall or cascade units. Like prefabricated pools, these are moulded in plastic or fibreglass and are available in both natural and unnatural colours. They are simple to install, for all that is required is that they be level from side to side, and with the lip protruding sufficiently to enable the full body of water to be emptied into the pool rather than on to the surrounding ground. The hose from the outlet of the pump is then carefully hidden, but emerges at the summit of the unit and the water gently tumbles down.

A waterfall does not have to be prefabricated to be successful and in certain circumstances it is desirable that it is not so. Prefabricated units are not necessarily of the shape or length desired and, when something special is needed, the waterfall can be made with concrete, although some suppliers suggest that a presentable feature can be constructed using a pool-liner. While this may be possible, it can by no stretch of the imagination be deemed easy.

A purpose-built waterfall will obviously have to conform visually to the site and fulfil its function of delivering water

[*Text continues on p. 48*

Water lily (*Nymphaea pygmaea* 'Rubra').
Although one of the dwarf water lilies, the
blooms and leaves of this variety are, in
fact, larger than the rest of the pygmy
forms. The flowers open rose in colour,
the outer petals being lightly flushed with
pink, and eventually change to a rich
garnet red.

The water lily (*Nymphaea* × *marliacea* 'Carnea'). Medium sized and suitable for depths of water 45–90 cm (1½–3 ft). The deep pink buds open into 10–12·5 cm (4–5 in) diameter flowers, which fade gradually to cream white.

from a higher area to a pool below. The upper part, or header pool, should be reasonably deep, but will not be capable of supporting aquatic plant life nor fish. Each small basin forming the cascade should be so constructed that, when the water is switched off, a small quantity remains in each. This can be done by tipping the leading edge up, so that water only flows over the lip when a reasonable quantity is being pumped. Concrete of the same consistency as is used for pool construction is used to form the waterfall which, like the pool, benefits from being 15 cm (6 in) deep. While the concrete is still wet, a more natural effect can be created by the addition of rockwork set into the concrete to create the faces of each small basin. This rockwork can similarly be used around the edges to hide their harshness. It is important that these edges be level in the horizontal plane so that water is distributed evenly throughout each basin.

Waterfalls of various kinds can be constructed that vary considerably from the traditional form. One of the most interesting of these is the grotto, where a pool is constructed with a background of similar appearance to a rock garden. A small cavern is constructed at the summit and contains a pump outlet surrounded by well-washed pebbles or cobbles. These stones extend down the watercourse, over which water flows with the aid of a simple submersible pump. The illusion is that the water is emerging from within the grotto. When tastefully dressed with ferns and other moisture-loving plants around its edges, it makes a very attractive if somewhat mystical feature.

From modesty to exuberance and one can scarcely get more exuberant than a water-staircase. Beloved of French

[Text continues on p. 52

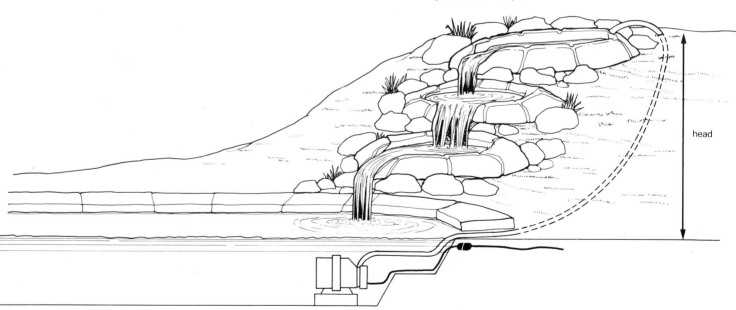

Fig. 9. Preformed waterfall.
Waterfall or cascade units can be made of plastic or fibreglass. They are simple to install; all that is required that they be level from side to side, and with the lip of the lowest basin protruding sufficiently so that the water empties directly into the pool water and not on to the edging of the pool.

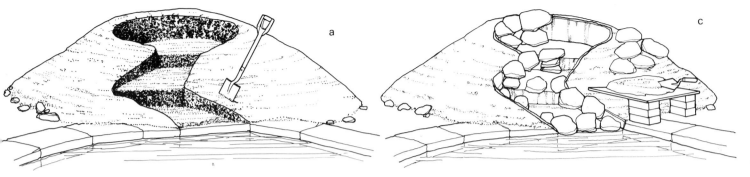

Fig. 10. Waterfall construction using a liner.
A waterfall constructed with a pool liner offers greater flexibility in design than does a preformed unit. It is, however, much more difficult to construct and you would be well advised to seek professional help in making this feature.

(*a*) On soil that is well consolidated, cut out the steps of the watercourse as required.

(*c*) Stones, bedded on mortar, are then laid down to form the watercourse. The positioning of the stones will determine the type of fall. Further stones can then be added around the edges to create a natural-looking watercourse. Finally, the surrounding ground on either side of the waterfall can be made into a rockery, thus completing the feature.

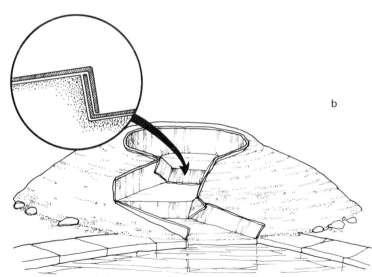

(*b*) Lay the liner into the excavated watercourse. The sides of the liner must be kept above the anticipated maximum water level. Each small basin forming the cascade should be so constructed that, when the water is switched off, a small quantity remains in each.

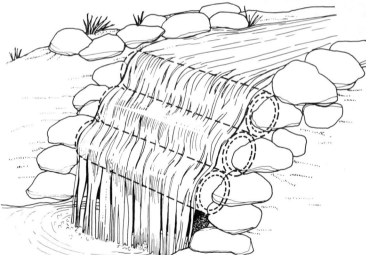

Fig. 11. Water staircase.
A mini-version of the latter-day water staircase beloved of French and Italian gardeners. Here the staircase is achieved by sizeable concrete drainage pipes set in a bed of concrete one behind the other, each pipe slightly above the next. To camouflage the ends, fill them with concrete or soil and then cover them with plants or rocks.

49

Golden club (*Orontium aquaticum*). Native to North America. A handsome aquatic suitable for deep or shallow water provided it has full sun. In shallow water the plant grows to a height of 30–45 cm (1–1½ ft); in deep water the leaves float. The yellow flowers appear in late spring and early summer, studding the tops of the white, pencil-thick stems.

The double marsh marigold (*Caltha palustris* 'Flore Pleno') growing at the water's edge at the foot of a scree garden. This beautiful, double-flowered form produces such an abundance of blooms as to hide the foliage; it grows about 30 cm (1 ft) tall. The rich golden flowers are about 2·5 cm (1 in) across (p. 61).

and Italian gardeners years ago, this feature can be tastefully recreated in the small garden. The idea behind a water-staircase is that it appears as a staircase of sparkling, silvery water. This can be achieved in the modern garden by the use of sizeable concrete drainage pipes set in a bed of concrete one behind the other, each pipe slightly above the next. Thus one has a staircase with rounded steps, but to disguise the edges it is necessary to fill the hollow ends of the pipes with concrete or soil and suitably hide them with plants. If the pipes are new, they may require treating with a pool-sealant.

The effect of a water-staircase can be marvellous, but only when sufficient water is flowing over it. If such a feature is envisaged, do not skimp on the purchase of a pump of sufficient size. The whole concept depends upon the volume of water being sufficient.

Filters

While most pumps have filters attached to their input, in order to gather debris and algae that are likely to cause mechanical problems, it is perfectly possible to fit further units to most classes of submersible pump to extract water-discolouring algae. These units should not, however, be used in an attempt to replace the natural balance between various kinds of aquatic plant, for this is the perfect answer for any pool. However, temporary problems do arise and then a filter can undoubtedly assist, particularly in the smaller pool where a natural balance is more difficult to establish.

The pool-filter usually looks like a deep tray. In fact, it is two trays, one inside the other, the inner one containing a foam filter element which is covered with gravel or charcoal. The pump is connected through the outer tray and draws water in through the gravel or charcoal, and then through the filter element into the pump for discharge as a fountain or waterfall. Debris and algae collect in the medium in the inner tray and can regularly be changed and disposed of. Another system uses a small filter, or algae trap, at the discharge side of the pump. The filter must be regularly changed.

Not all filters operate as successfully as their manufacturers claim, so they should be purchased with great caution. In order to ensure that the filter functions correctly, the retailer should be willing to arrange a demonstration of it in operation. A filter is an unsightly adjunct to the pool, but this can to some extent be disregarded if it is functional.

4 Planting the Pool

Water gardening is unlike any other kind of gardening, for when planting a pool the gardener is creating a whole new underwater world in which plants, fish and snails depend upon one another to provide the basic requirements necessary for their continued existence. Submerged oxygenating plants replace the oxygen that has been lost in respiration. They compete with slimes, algae and other primitive forms of plant life, which turn the water thick and green, by using up all the available mineral salts. The slimes and algae are thus starved out of existence. Floating plants assist by shading the surface of the water and making life intolerable for any of the green water-discolouring algae which try to dwell beneath them. Water lilies and marginal plants, of limited value in maintaining a balance, provide the necessary colour to make the pool a continual source of pleasure and delight.

Submerged oxygenating plants

Submerged oxygenating plants are those that we affectionately refer to as 'weeds', and their function is to maintain healthy, well-oxygenated water for the fish and other livestock. However, from the gardener's point of view they serve another purpose too, for all thrive on the same mineral salts as green water-discolouring algae and, being more advanced forms of plant life, they are able to starve the algae out and ensure crystal-clear water if planted in sufficient numbers at the outset.

Submerged oxygenating plants are usually sold as bunches of unrooted cuttings, fastened together at the base with a strip of lead. Although appearing to be clinging precariously to life, once introduced to the pool they quickly produce roots and become established. Apart from fastening the cuttings together, the lead strip acts as a weight to hold the bunch down. It is important when planting submerged oxygenating plants that this lead weight is buried in the compost, or else it will rot through the stems and they will come floating to the surface. Some pool-owners plant their submerged plants in containers full of pea gravel, but trays or proper planting containers of good clean heavy soil, topped off with a generous layer of pea gravel to prevent fish from stirring the mud up and fouling the water, are best.

There are a whole host of submerged oxygenating plants to choose from, but it is generally conceded that the common fish weed (*Lagarosiphon major*) is the best kind for most situations. This is the thick, dark green, snake-like submerged plant popularly sold by pet shops for goldfish bowls and aquaria. It is almost evergreen, a strong grower, yet not invasive. Canadian pondweed (*Elodea canadensis*) is the species with a bad reputation that is seldom deserved. It is true that, in a situation to its liking, it will rapidly form colonies of underwater growth, but in the average garden pool excessive growth can be easily controlled by hand. Although not exceptionally attractive, it does have its charm, the thick forests of dark olive green foliage persisting for much of the year.

For an elegant submerged oxygenating plant we have to look to our native water violet (*Hottonia palustris*). During late spring this little beauty thrusts up stout stems which hold aloft delicate, pale lilac blossoms above handsome whorls of finely divided, apple-green foliage. The water crowfoot (*Ranunculus aquatilis*) also produces its flowers above the surface of the water, glistening white-and-gold chalices borne amongst dark green, floating, clover-like leaves which bear little resemblance to the flaccid, deeply dissected submerged foliage. The milfoils have dense whorls of feathery foliage, the spiked milfoil (*Myriophyllum spicatum*) and whorled milfoil (*M. verticillatum*) being the most

[*Text continues on p. 56*

Yellow flag (*Iris pseudacorus*). A marginal aquatic that will grow in marshy ground or shallow water. It has 7–8 cm (3–3½ in) rich yellow flowers on 60–90 cm (2–3 ft) stems and sword-like leaves. It is a bulky plant and cannot be recommended for the very small pool (p. 61).

54

Blue iris (*Iris laevigata*). Native to
Manchuria, Korea and Japan. One of the
best blue-flowered aquatics for early
summer, the plant does equally well in
shallow water or boggy ground. It grows
60–75 cm (2–2½ ft) tall with strap-shaped
leaves and bears large 10–15 cm (4–6 in)
rich blue flowers.

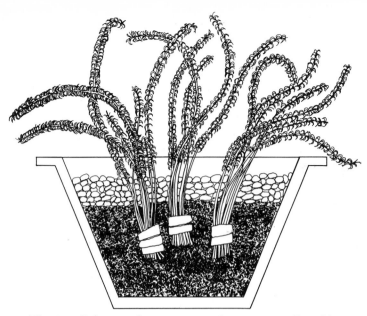

Fig. 12. Submerged oxygenating plants are usually sold as bunches of uprooted cuttings, fastened together at the base with a strip of lead, which acts as a weight to hold them down. The lead weight should be buried in the compost, otherwise it will rot through the stems and the plants will float to the surface.

attractive and excellent plants for goldfish to spawn in. Other submerged oxygenating plants worth considering include the starworts, hornworts and willow moss.

Floating plants

Floating aquatics have a different way of life to anything the gardener commonly encounters. Not only do they infrequently produce roots for anchorage or absorption of plant foods, but most develop turions, or winter buds, and effectively disappear for the winter. The water chestnut (*Trapa natans*) is a prime example, although it does not so much retreat into a bud, but rather overwinters as a spiny nut or seed. It is one of the most attractive floating aquatics, during the summer months sporting rosettes of dark green rhomboidal leaves and creamy-white axillary blossoms.

The frogbit (*Hydrocharis morsus-ranae*) forms a tiny bud in the autumn and seldom reappears until early summer. For this reason it is wise to keep a few in a bowl during the winter, so that they can be given a little warmth during early spring to encourage premature growth and help shade the first flush of water-discolouring algae. Allowed to remain in the cool waters of the pool, they take a considerable time to reappear and fulfil their role, and often fall prey to browsing water snails. With its neat and attractive rosettes of kidney-shaped leaves and papery-white, three-petalled flowers, it is an ideal aquatic for the smaller pool or sink garden, and a much better proposition than the closely related water soldier (*Stratiotes aloides*). Not that we should despise this curious native; it is just that it can attain a considerable size and, in favourable conditions, increases rapidly by means of runners. It is usually well behaved though, a strong floating plant with bronze-green spiny foliage, which looks very much like a pineapple top, and has delicate white flowers.

However, the best floating aquatic of all is not completely hardy and is usually replaced each year. The water hyacinth (*Eichhornia crassipes*) makes a bold display from early summer until the first autumn frost reduces it to pulp. Bold spikes of lilac-and-yellow, orchid-like blossoms are produced amongst glossy green leaves with grotesquely inflated leaf bases which give the plant buoyancy. It is an easy-going plant that increases freely from runners, the young plants being easily overwintered in a pan of wet soil in a frost-free greenhouse.

Water lilies

As one can well imagine, the surface shade so necessary for a healthy balance within the pool can also be provided by water lilies. However, this is not the main reason for gardeners wishing to grow these gorgeous subjects, for throughout the summer they provide a dazzling display of beautifully sculptured blossoms in almost every shape, size and colour imaginable. There are pygmy varieties that can be grown in a sink, right through to vigorous kinds that are only suited to a lake or large pool in a public park.

The dwarf or pygmy kinds grow in as little as 15 cm (6 in) to 23 cm (9 in) of water, rarely spreading more than 30 cm (1 ft) across and with tiny flowers that are in proportion. The tiny white *Nymphaea pygmaea* 'Alba' and canary-yellow *N.*

[*Text continues on p. 60*

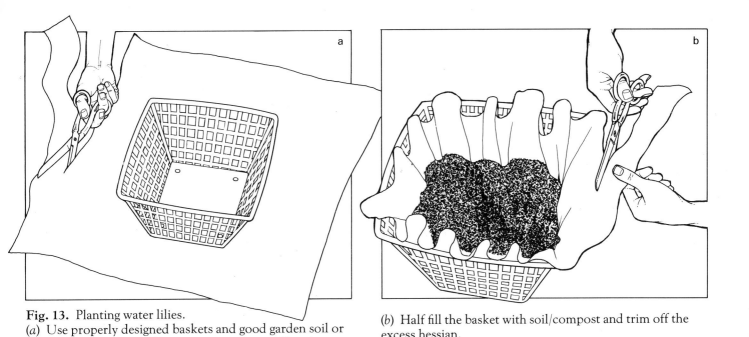

Fig. 13. Planting water lilies.
(*a*) Use properly designed baskets and good garden soil or a heavy loam compost. First cut out a square of hessian to line the planting basket.

(*b*) Half fill the basket with soil/compost and trim off the excess hessian.

(*c*) Plant the lily in the soil/compost.

(*d*) Continue to fill the basket with soil/compost to within an inch or so of the top, and then cover with a layer of pea shingle.

A striking bog garden plant *Lysichitum camstschatcense*. Native to Japan, it grows to a height of 60–90 cm (2–3 ft). The large leaves have pointed tips and long, sheath-like stalks. The flowers consist of a pure white, open spathe enclosing a central green spike (spadix).

Opposite: The pickerel (*Pontaderia cordata*). A decorative marginal plant that extends the flowering season well into the autumn with its small purple-blue flowers carried amidst glossy green foliage. The plant grows in water up to 23 cm (9 in) deep; height 45–75 cm (1½–2½ ft).

pygmaea 'Helvola' are the most popular of these, although there are both red and pink varieties available. The *laydekeri* group of water lilies require slightly deeper water, but nevertheless are invaluable for the small pool. *Nymphaea laydekeri* 'Purpurata' has wine-red petals and orange stamens, 'Lilacea' carmine flowers which age to deep plum, and 'Alba' has pure white blossoms with an overpowering fragrance of fresh tea.

A similar group of hybrids are suitable for greater depths of up to 90 cm (3 ft). These are known as the *marliacea* types and characterized by the very popular *N. marliacea* 'Chromatella' with soft yellow blooms amidst dark olive green foliage which is heavily splashed and stained with maroon. The variety 'Flammea' has similar foliage but fiery red flowers, while both 'Rosea' and 'Carnea' have plain green leaves as a foil to their rose and soft pink blossoms.

Outside the main water lily groups there are innumerable hybrids of equal merit: the lovely deep pink 'Firecrest' with its bold purplish foliage, the icy-white 'Albatross' and deep red 'Froebeli'. 'Amabilis' has striking star-shaped, salmon-pink blossoms, 'Gonnêre' fully double, globular flowers like huge white snowballs, while 'Aurora' is the best of the chameleon varieties, its blooms passing from yellow, through orange to blood-red with each succeeding day.

Like all aquatic plants, water lilies can be planted successfully from spring until late summer, using properly designed baskets and good garden soil. It is important when collecting soil to avoid getting any old leaves or weeds mixed in with it, as these will only decompose and foul the water. Soil from land that has been recently dressed with artificial fertilizer should be similarly avoided, as this too will pollute the water. Plant the water lily with just the 'nose', or growing point, protruding above the soil and then cover the surface of the basket with a generous layer of pea gravel to prevent the fish from stirring up the mud. Before putting the water lily in the pool, soak the basket thoroughly with water from a watering can fitted with a fine rose. This will drive most of the air out of the growing medium and prevent clouds of bubbles and associated debris from being released into the pool. It is also useful to remove all the adult leaves from water lilies (or indeed any lily-like aquatics) before planting, as these give the plants buoyancy and can lift them out of the basket. When placing water lilies in the pool, it is essential to situate them well away from a fountain or waterfall and in a really sunny position, for they are intolerant of shade or turbulent water.

Although water lilies are the most important group of deep-water aquatics, they do not have an automatic right to the deeper areas of the pool. There are a number of other deep-water aquatics well worth considering for this.

Deep-water aquatics

The water hawthorn (*Aponogeton distachyus*) is undisputedly the most valuable decorative aquatic, apart from the water lilies, for the modern pool. A modest fellow with dark green, more or less oblong leaves which are often splashed and spotted with purple. It is a perfect foil for the display of white, vanilla-scented blossoms with jet-black stamens which continue from early spring until the first severe frost.

Pond lilies, or nuphars, need regarding with caution, even though they are regularly sold for the garden pool and look most attractive in their young state. Many, like our native brandy bottle (*Nuphar lutea*) are extremely invasive and only suited to farm ponds. However, the diminutive *N. pumila* is well worth considering for the smaller pool, for its crispy, membranous underwater foliage alone. It also produces modest, bright green floating leaves and myriad tiny golden blossoms.

The water fringe (*Nymphoides peltata*) should also receive consideration. Often dubbed the 'poor man's water lily', it has a manner of growth which suggests to the uninitiated that it might be a pygmy water lily: handsome, bright green, rounded foliage, occasionally splashed with brown, and delicate yellow, fringed, buttercup-like blossoms that make a show for much of the summer. For the keen gardener though there is the golden club (*Orontium aquaticum*). A curious member of the arum lily family, this bizarre aquatic makes a bold display of golden, pencil-like flowers during late spring and early summer. It is an easy-going character that is, strictly speaking, a deep-water aquatic, but grows equally well in mud at the water's edge if you are unable to provide ideal conditions.

Marginal plants

Like the golden club, most aquatic plants are reasonably adaptable as to the depth of water in which they will prosper, as most have to contend with widely fluctuating water levels and consequently have little objection to growing in wet mud or up to 23 cm (9 in) of water. Marginal plants, as their name implies, grow in the shallow water at the pool's edge and can either be grown in planting baskets, like water lilies, or in soil that has been placed directly on the marginal shelf. This latter proposition is not ideal as the more rampant plants will crowd out the less vigorous and often more desirable subjects.

There are many different marginal plants to choose from, but most pool-owners have a strong affection for the aquatic irises. These are usually represented by the blue iris of the Asian paddy fields (*Iris laevigata*), or else our rather bulky native yellow flag (*I. pseudacorus*). Both species have variegated foliage varieties and hybrid forms that are much improved. 'Rose Queen' and 'Snowdrift' are amongst the best varieties of *I. laevigata*, while 'Golden Queen' is a great improvement upon the common flag, although it cannot be recommended for the very small pool.

Everyone likes to see the brown, poker-like heads of the reed maces beside their pool, but great care must be taken to select the less invasive *Typha stenophylla* or the diminutive Japanese *T. minima*. Our native reed maces are much too vigorous and will swamp a small pool very quickly. These are the plants that are popularly referred to as 'bulrushes', but in fact they are not. The true bulrush is *Scirpus lacustris*, a handsome plant with dark green, needle-like rushes that give the average pool much-needed height and help to soften its often harsh outline. Together with its creamy white-and-green striped counterparts 'Albescens' and 'Zebrinus', it completes the array of rushes that can be safely recommended for the modern water garden, except for the flowering rush (*Butomus umbellatus*). This is not technically a rush and produces umbels of rose-pink flowers during late summer. In fact, it is more closely allied to the arrowhead.

The arrowhead (*Sagittaria japonica*) has broad, green, arrow-shaped leaves and sprays of pure white flowers with conspicuous golden centres, while its improved double form 'Flore Pleno' has snow-white blooms like miniature powder puffs. The bog bean (*Menyanthes trifoliata*) flowers during early spring with quaint pinkish-white fringed blooms amongst dark green foliage like that of a broad bean. This associates well with the common marsh marigold (*Caltha palustris*) and its equally lovely golden yellow, fully double-flowered form 'Flore Pleno'. There is a single white variety named *alba* and an enormous bright yellow cousin from the Himalayas called *C. polypetala*.

Another bright group of plants are the monkey musks, many of which are usually grown in a damp position in the herbaceous border. All grow well in the shallows of a pool, along with their truly aquatic neighbour *Mimulus ringens*, an easily grown kind with spires of glossy green foliage and attractive lavender-blue flowers. The water forget-me-not (*Myosotis scorpioides*) also enjoys shallow water. It has slightly less hairy leaves, but otherwise looks identical to the familiar bedding forget-me-not. Unlike the ordinary kind, this is a perennial and will continue from year to year. It is also much later flowering, but will continue to do so until the autumn frosts. The water plantain (*Alisma plantago-aquatica*) has large spreading panicles of pinkish flowers which remain as fine upstanding skeletons throughout the winter, while the water mint (*Mentha aquatica*) has strongly aromatic foliage sprinkled with fluffy balls of lilac-pink flowers.

The bog arum (*Calla palustris*) produces pure white spathes like tiny sails amongst glossy, heart-shaped foliage, and in autumn is covered in clusters of rich mahogany-red berries. Where space allows, the American skunk cabbage (*Lysichitum americanum*) can be grown. This has huge yellow spathes which appear during early spring long before its handsome silvery foliage. Its Japanese counterpart (*L. camtschatcense*) is equally free flowering, but with white flowers that are slightly smaller and usually a couple of weeks later. While it may seem that most of the marginal plants are of summer duration, the pickerel (*Pontederia cordata*) extends the flowering season well into autumn with its spikes of small, delphinium-blue flowers amidst striking glossy green foliage. Indeed, with careful planning, there can always be colour at the poolside from early spring until the first autumn frosts.

Left: Plantain lily (*Hosta sieboldii albomarginata*). Native to Japan. A bog garden plant with bold, white-margined leaves which make the plant attractive even when not in bloom. It has lilac flowers, up to thirty on a stem. Height 75 cm (2½ ft).

Right: Another species of plantain lily, *Hosta elata*, again native in Japan. A robust plant, forming mounds of dark green leaves, these having wavy margins. Flowers are pale blue/violet in colour and are each about 5 cm (2 in) in length. The plant grows to a height of 90 cm (3 ft).

While most gardeners wish to grow as many aquatic plants as they can comfortably accommodate, water is in itself an attractive feature, and sufficient uncluttered area must be allowed for reflections. An overplanted pool detracts from its surroundings, while it should essentially be a feature that complements them. Spotty or regimented planting cannot be tolerated either. Marginal plants in particular should be grouped together like plants in an herbaceous border, several of the same variety being accommodated in a single basket. Apart from being aesthetically undesirable to have mixed plantings, it is impractical too, for the more vigorous plants outgrow their weaker neighbours and create difficulties.

Bog garden plants

It is always difficult to know where aquatic plants end, bog plants begin, and ordinary herbaceous border plants take over. As a rough-and-ready guide, bog plants can be considered to be any subjects which like moist conditions but not standing water, and if treated as ordinary border plants become stunted and the foliage scorched.

Plantain lilies, or hostas, are good examples of what one might term true bog garden plants, looking sad and weary in a dryish border, but flourishing in a moist organic medium. The leaves are, of course, their chief delight, but one must not overlook the grace and charm of their not insignificant pendant blossoms. The commonest variety is *Hosta undulata medio-variegata* with slightly twisted variegated leaves in a conglomeration of cream, green and white. The hybrid 'Thomas Hogg' is a little more orderly with plain green leaves with a white marginal band, while one of its illustrious parents, *H. lancifolia*, has given rise to the most outstanding golden-leafed variety called 'Aurea' and the enormous 'Fortis'. *Hosta glauca* is a very common kind with large, heart-shaped, steely blue-green leaves, while *H. fortunei* is noted for its attractive spikes of pendent, funnel-shaped, lilac blossoms.

Moisture-loving irises add height with their handsome swordlike foliage, particularly the taller-growing kinds like *Iris ochraleuca* and *I. ochraurea*. However, these can be rather overbearing in the small garden and are better replaced by the Japanese clematis-flowered iris (*I. kaempferi*) and its cousin *I. sibirica*. Both are of modest proportions, yet produce blooms of great substance and quality during midsummer, particularly *I. kaempferi* with gorgeous blossoms like delicate tropical butterflies at rest amongst slender grassy foliage.

Astilbes provide interest during high summer with their neat mounds of green foliage and brightly coloured, feathery plumes of flowers. Innumerable hybrids are available covering a wide colour range, the bright crimson 'Fanal', salmon-pink 'Peach Blossom' and 'White Gloria' being three that embrace the important areas occupied by the astilbe. The meadow sweets also revel in wet areas, the double form of our common meadow sweet (*Filipendula ulmaria*) being especially attractive and well complemented by the equally garden-worthy foliage kind 'Aurea'.

Bog garden primulas exhibit a diversity seldom found in other groups of plants and can be flowering from very early spring through until the frosts of early autumn. The drumstick primula (*Primula denticulata*) in lilac, rose or white opens the season, together with the tiny rose-pink *P. rosea* and its more prolific progeny 'Micia de Geer'. Candelabra varieties follow, mixed hybrids like 'Harlow Car Hybrids' being superb, but it is species such as the bright orange *P. aurantiaca* that lead the procession. The crimson *P. japonica* and its cultivars 'Miller's Crimson' and 'Postford White' are close on its heels, together with the deep rosy-purple *P. burmanica* and the handsome mealy-stemmed and magenta-blossoming *P. pulverulenta*. The rich jaffa-orange *P. bulleyana* brings up the rear, extending the season well into summer, while the tall and beautiful Himalayan cowslip (*P. florindae*) may persist with its pendant sulphurous bells until early autumn.

The globe flowers or *Trollius* are like giant buttercups and liven up the pool or streamside during early spring, while for moist places that are not truly bog but continuously moist, some of the lovely bell-flowered uvularias can be tried. The tallest is the North American *Uvularia grandiflora*, its delicate pendent bells of rich yellow presenting a picture of unparalleled beauty when planted at the poolside and reflected in the mirror-like surface of the water.

5 FISH AND OTHER LIVESTOCK

Fish and other livestock are essential in maintaining a healthy environment in the pool. Indeed, they are essential for the control of aquatic insect life (which otherwise disfigures aquatic plants) and the larvae of the mosquito, the adults of which plague the gardener on summer evenings. They are also much valued as an additional source of interest in the water garden, adding colour and life to the pool and providing entertainment for old and young alike.

Ornamental pool fish that are commonly sold to the pond-owner usually live amicably together, irrespective of size or species. The only difficult character is the catfish, which during its formative life feeds upon aquatic insect life, but which will turn its attention to small fish and the tails of larger ones as it reaches maturity. Once introduced to a pool it is very difficult to catch without draining the water away, and then it resists capture, squirming about in the mud and debris on the pool floor. Providing that the catfish is avoided, and no more than a total of 15 cm (6 in) length of fish is introduced for every 0·09 square metre (square foot) of the surface area of the deep parts, then few problems should be encountered. This is a *maximum* stocking rate. If the fish are required to grow and breed, then a stocking rate of one-third of that, or 5 cm (2 in) of fish to every 0·09 square metre (square foot) of surface area, is more satisfactory. The size of individual fish is not important. It is the total combination of body length upon which the formula is based.

Ornamental pond fish

Goldfish are the obvious choice when stocking a new pool, becoming tame when fed regularly from the hand and providing a diversity of colour and shape not encountered in any other group of coldwater fish. The conventional goldfish is familiar to all, a red or bright orange carp-type varying in length from a couple of inches to 30 cm (1 ft) or more. The difference in size is not, as many suppose, due to variation within the species, but governed by the space available to the fish. That is why a goldfish confined to a round bowl for a number of years retains its small size, yet once introduced to a pool will grow rapidly and attain quite sizeable proportions.

Apart from obvious variations in colour, the most striking divergence from the true goldfish is the transparent-scaled variety: the shubunkin. In this, the body appears smooth and scaleless, and in richly varied colour combinations. Blues, yellows, reds and violet intermingle with one another and are often splashed and stained with black or crimson. Comet longtailed forms of both shubunkins and goldfish occur, the tails of these selections being almost as long as the body and giving the appearance of a comet.

Fantails and moors are also forms of goldfish, but with short, rounded bodies and handsome, divided tails. They are not quite so robust as the ordinary goldfish, but their exceptional beauty makes them hard to resist. A number possess the rainbow hues of the shubunkin, while others are red or red-and-white, but the most gorgeous of all is the black moor, a velvety-black fantail with telescopic eyes. In addition, there is the somewhat bizarre celestial with its staring upturned eyes; the appropriately named bubble-eye; and those two fish-fancier delights, the oranda and lionhead.

Carp are close relatives of the goldfish. Indeed, the goldfish itself is technically a member of the carp family, and is available in a multitude of varieties. Most are coarse, bulky native fish, suited to large pools and lakes, but of dull appearance and rather too boisterous for the garden pool. Two exceptions are the Chinese red carp, or Higoi, and the Japanese Nishiki Koi which is popularly known just as Koi. The Higoi is thought to be a variation of the common carp,

[Text continues on p. 68

Candelabra primrose (*Primula pulverulenta*), a dainty bog garden plant, from West China. The whorls of magenta/crimson flowers, carried on stems reaching 60–90 cm (2–3 ft), appear in early summer.

The drumstick primrose (*Primula denticulata*). Smaller than *P. pulverulenta*, growing to only 30–60 cm (1–2 ft), this bog garden plant is nevertheless of robust growth. The leaves grow in rosettes and the large crowded heads of pale lavender flowers appear in early spring.

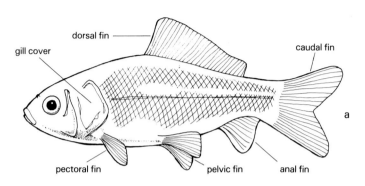

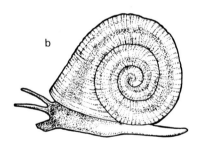

Fig. 14. Livestock.
(*a*) Goldfish are the obvious choice when stocking a new pool. They provide a diversity of colour and shape not encountered in any other group of coldwater fish.

(*b*) Scavenging snail: the ramshorn. This humble mollusc can be unreservedly recommended as it is hardy and lives exclusively on algae.

but with a depressed head and orange, pink or salmon colouration, whereas the Nishiki Koi is even finer and derived from the interbreeding of several different species of carp over hundreds of years. Named varieties, some with metallic mirror-like scales are available in colours that range from violet and grey through the reds and orange to yellow and white, or else in combinations of two or more of these colours. 'Shiro-ogen' is white, 'Sanke' white with red-and-black markings, 'Ki-ogen', yellow, and 'Bekko', tortoise-shell.

Goldfish and carp varieties, although the most brilliantly coloured ornamental pond fish, always occupy the middle zone of the pool, only coming to the surface to feed or sunbathe. Golden orfe are more visible, swimming in shoals just beneath the surface of the water, and playfully splashing and snatching unwary insects from the air. They are slender fish with deep orange-pink backs and silvery bellies which, under favourable conditions, may attain a length in excess of 45 cm (18 in).

Scavenging fish and snails

At the other end of the scale, there are the scavenging fish which grub about on the floor of the pool and are seldom seen. The green tench is the most useful, devouring all manner of aquatic insect larvae and clearing up any uneaten fish food which falls to the bottom. Coldwater catfish are often recommended for this task, but are totally unsuited as, unlike many of their tropical counterparts, they are exclusively carnivorous, preying on snails, goldfish fry or any other unsuspecting small fish.

It is a popular misconception that, if a couple of tench are put in a pool, they will clear it of algae and scud along the bottom like a vacuum cleaner, devouring organic matter, mud, stones and anything else that gets in their way. In fact, a pool can function quite well without scavenging fish, although unquestionably their presence is beneficial.

When stocking a pool with fish, take care to select healthy individuals with firm, meaty bodies and erect dorsal fins. It is important to wait until the plants have had time to become well-established before introducing the fish, otherwise they will uproot the plants and dirty the water, and the entire pool will then go green as the uprooted plants are unable to function.

Patience is also necessary before introducing freshwater snails or mussels, as both require mature water if they are to thrive. Of the aquatic snails, only the ramshorns can be unreservedly recommended. The other hardy species are not exclusively algae-eating and feed to some extent upon decorative plants within the pool. The ramshorn is quite a distinctive fellow with a somewhat flattened shell which the creature carries in an upright fashion on its back, a complete contrast to the other commonly available, but much less desirable species, the freshwater whelk, or greater pond snail. This and the majority of other hardy water snails have tall, spiralled and pointed shells and greyish, fleshy bodies.

While aquatic snails feed predominantly upon filamentous algae, the freshwater mussels consume large quantities of the free-floating kind, sucking in and blowing out water and retaining all manner of minute suspended life. For mussels to be happy, the pool should be well-established with a reasonable covering of organic matter on the floor in which they can shuffle. The painter's mussel and swan mussel are the two species commonly available, the former being the more decorative, the latter the more functional.

Breeding a few fish

Most pool-owners are thrilled if they can persuade their fish to breed successfully. All the fish that the average person is likely to have are of the carp family and have similar requirements for their successful reproduction, although certain species, such as orfe and tench, seem loath to breed in captivity in Britain. However, all the fish known collectively as carp and, of course, the common goldfish and its forms reproduce freely, and many interbreed with one another.

The breeding season lasts from late spring until late summer, depending to some degree upon temperature. Most goldfish and related fish are sexually mature in their second year, although adulthood is related more directly to size than age. Any goldfish 8 cm (3 in) or more in length should be capable of breeding. Most pool-owners who wish to breed a few fish start by purchasing one or two matched pairs and, while this can be recommended, it does not follow that the pair purchased will breed with one another if there are other sizeable fish in the pool. Generally, like will breed with like, but hybrids in the carp family are common, and those of similar shape and constitution do interbreed.

Identifying the male and female fish is relatively easy in the spring. Body shape, when viewed from above, is oval and elliptical for the female, and slim and pencil-like for the male, the male being further enhanced by white, pimple-like nuptial tubercles which are sprinkled over the gill covers and top of the head.

Spawning takes place with varying frequency throughout the breeding season. During spawning the male fish chases the female around the pool and amongst the submerged plants, brushing and pushing furiously against her flanks. She then releases the spawn, trailing it in and amongst the stems and foliage of submerged plant life. The male milt, or sperm-bearing fluid, is distributed over the eggs which are then hopefully fertilized. Once this has happened, it is advisable to remove some of the plant material covered in spawn away from the preying adults (who will promptly eat most of it if there is only sparse plant cover in the pool). It can be placed in a cool environment in an aquarium with pond water until the young fry are large enough to survive the rough-and-tumble of the garden pool. It is important to use *pond* water in the aquarium, as this is the only medium which will be compatible to the spawn.

After three or four days the fry will be seen developing. First of all, they are difficult to detect as they are minute and resemble tiny pins clinging to the leaves and stems of submerged plants. After a couple of weeks they are recognizable as fish, sometimes transparent, sometimes bronze, but all eventually attaining their correct adult proportions and colours.

There are few problems for the pool-owner with a desire to breed a few fish, particularly if he starts with healthy stock of good conformation. Indeed, if goldfish and carp are placed in a pool, providing that the proportion of males and females is reasonably balanced, they will probably breed with some measure of success of their own accord without the pool-owner needing to become involved.

Candelabra primrose (*Primula bulleyana*). Another bog-garden plant from West China, having similar characteristics to *P. pulverulenta*. The plant grows to 60–90 cm (2–3 ft), has thin, papery leaves and buff-orange flowers approximately 2 cm ($\frac{3}{4}$ in) across.

Astilbe (*Astilbe × arendsii* 'Bressingham Beauty'). Astilbes may be grown in herbaceous borders as well as bog-garden plants beside a pool. This variety has deep green foliage, grows to 60–90 cm (2–3 ft) and bears a profusion of minute, pink flowers.

6 POOL MAINTENANCE

Establishing a water garden is initially time-consuming, but once properly planted and stocked it is relatively undemanding compared with many other features of the garden. Routine care consists of keeping an eye open for pests and diseases, and lifting and dividing water lilies every third or fourth year and marginal plants alternate years. The latter are divided in much the same way as ordinary border plants immediately they become crowded, but water lilies are slightly different and require a certain amount of care. Evidence of the need to divide water lilies in an established clump is the preponderance of leaf growth in the centre of the plant accompanied by diminishing flower size. With most varieties, the time to divide comes along every three or four years, although some of the smaller hybrids may go on for as long as six or seven years without requiring attention.

Dividing water lilies

Late spring is the ideal time to divide water lilies, the plants being lifted and the adult foliage removed at source. Most plants consist of a main rootstock from which several 'eyes' have grown to form sizeable 'branches', and it is these side growths that should be retained, cutting them from the parent with as much healthy young rootstock as possible. The thick bulky part of the original plant is generally of little use and should be discarded, but all the 'branches' can be planted individually to form new plants, providing that they each have a healthy terminal shoot.

Submerged oxygenating plants sometimes encroach beyond reasonable bounds and these too should be dealt with regularly. Many pool-owners pull plants up by the handful and then wonder why the water turns green. Obviously, this is because the natural balance has been disturbed. A much more satisfactory method is to reduce the bushy foliage by about a third with a sharp knife or a pair of scissors. If the adult plants are looking weary, then these can be removed, the severed stems picked over, the healthiest pieces bunched together with a strip of lead or piece of wire, and then replanted in the vacant baskets.

Feeding aquatic plants

Feeding is an important factor in a successful pool. Water lilies and marginal aquatics are all gross feeders and require regular treatment if they are to prosper. Unfortunately, difficulty is often experienced in getting fertilizer down to the roots without lifting and replanting in fresh compost or otherwise considerably fouling the water. Special sachets of aquatic plant fertilizer are currently available which can be merely pushed into the container beside the plant. For those with a practical turn of mind it is a simple matter to make bonemeal 'pills' which are also pushed into the soil alongside the plants. These so-called 'pills' are made with a handful of coarse bonemeal and sufficient wet clay to bind it together.

The frequency with which the operation is carried out depends upon the plants involved and the compost or soil in which they were originally planted, but its need becomes apparent when the leaves of the plant become yellowish and get progressively smaller, and the blooms are of poor colour and with few petals. Marginal plants can benefit considerably from this treatment, but it should not be provided for those of a rampant nature. Submerged oxygenating plants and floating subjects gain most of their nourishment directly from water, so attempting to feed them is time consuming and undesirable.

Algae control

Apart from the nourishment of plant life, the only other important thing to consider is algae control. Although also discussed in Chapter 7, the presence of algae is not so much an intractable problem as a perennial hazard demanding continuous vigilance to control it. Aquatic algae occur in various forms, but notably free-floating and filamentous. The free-floating, or yellow-green kinds, are about the size of a pin-head and occur in their millions to create a green 'bloom' or the familiar pea soup effect. The filamentous algaes, on the other hand, appear as free-floating silkweed or *Spirogyra*, which can be dragged from the pool in handfuls, or else in thick mats known as blanket or flannel weed. Other kinds are fairly innocuous, like the mermaid's hair which clings to plant baskets and often coats the walls of the pool.

As intimated in Chapter 7, the control of algae on a temporary basis can be effected by chemical means, but this is always likely to be short-lived as the chemistry of the water is so susceptible to change. The most stable control is created by the theory of natural balance, the correct proportions of plant types and livestock for the given area. So it is important from the outset to see that plant types are always available in sufficient numbers to maintain a happy balance.

Preparing the pool for winter

Algae seldom pose any problems during winter, for then the pool becomes dull and lifeless, but the preparation for this period of dormancy is with most pool-owners a sadly neglected one. Untidy foliage at the water's edge provides a sanctuary for water lily beetles and other aquatic pests, so should be removed as soon as the first autumn frosts turn it brown. Care should be taken when trimming rushes with hollow stems, as these will 'drown' if cut below water level, so sufficient length should remain to allow for a fluctuating water level.

Water lilies can be allowed to die back naturally, but any leaves with soft, crumbling edges or spreading black blotches should be regarded with suspicion and removed, as they may well be infected by water lily leaf spot. This is not a deadly disease, but does spoil established water lilies. The new pool-owner will almost certainly feel some concern for his water lilies during the winter, but, providing they are growing in a suitable depth of water, they will overwinter perfectly. Miniature water lilies that may be growing in a shallow rock pool or sink should ideally have all the water drained off their crowns and then be protected by a generous layer of old leaves or straw. Once the danger of frost has passed, they can easily be restarted into growth by refilling the pool or sink with water. It is important to remember to cover the empty pool or sink in the autumn, or it will rapidly refill from rain and snow.

All desirable free-floating aquatic plants disappear for the winter months, forming turions, or winter buds, which fall to the bottom of the pool until the warm spring sunshine stirs them into growth once again. If these are collected before they sink and are placed in a jar of water in a cool airy place, they will start into growth much sooner and, by providing much needed surface shade, they can help to combat the troublesome algal growth that is almost invariably experienced in early spring.

Leaves from overhanging trees present a hazard during autumn and early winter. Netting the entire pool is a sensible precaution, although when leaves are merely blown in from surrounding areas a low wire netting fence supported by canes acts as a barrier. Leaves decomposing in the water, particularly of toxic species like horse chestnut, are one of the greatest dangers the fish keeper has to contend with.

Fish should be prepared for their winter vigil by judicious feeding with ants' eggs, dried flies or freeze-dried tubifex worms until the weather turns cold and they cease to be active. No further nourishment need be provided until they are seen swimming about once again in the spring. All popular kinds of decorative pond fish can survive for several months during the winter without feeding, as their body processes slow down in much the same manner as a tree or shrub in the garden becomes dormant. Likewise, they can stand extreme cold and will not suffer even if frozen beneath a layer of ice for a day or two.

Ice is the greatest worry that a pool-owner has during the winter months, for not only does it trap noxious gases which are likely to suffocate the fish, but it also exerts tremendous pressure upon the pool structure and can crack the most expertly laid concrete. The best way to prevent such damage occurring is to float a piece of wood or a child's rubber ball on the water, so that the ice exerts pressure against an object capable of expanding and contracting. If a submersible pump is used during the summer, then this can be detached and an electric pool-heater installed in its place. This consists of a heated brass rod with a polystyrene float, and is perfectly safe to use, keeping an area of water clear of ice in the severest weather. Alternatively, during a spell of prolonged cold weather when one fears for the safety of the fish, a hole can be made in the ice by placing a pan of boiling water on the surface and allowing this to melt through. Never make a hole in the ice by hitting it with a blunt instrument as this will kill or concuss the fish.

7 Pool Problems

As with most other living garden features the pool is not without its share of troubles. The commonest of these is undoubtedly discoloured water.

Discoloured water

Green water of a consistency like pea soup is familiar to most pool-owners, for even in well-established pools this condition may occur for a few days during early spring when the water is warmed by the sun, so algae appears before the submerged oxygenating plants have had a chance to start growing again.

It is the oxygenating plants that provide the key to the problem, for greenness in the water is caused by thousands of minute primitive free-floating algae feeding on the mineral salts that are present. When faced with competition from the higher forms of aquatic plant life, they die out through starvation, thus leaving the pool clear.

To ensure clarity from the outset, it is essential that earlier advice is followed when establishing a new pool. If an old-established one is causing problems, then the same advice applies. Plant one bunch of submerged oxygenating plant to every 0·185 sq metre (2 sq ft) of surface area and provide shade with floating plants and water lily pads over approximately one-third of the surface area. This latter effectively reduces the amount of sunlight falling directly into the water and generally makes conditions inhospitable for the growth of algae.

Algicides are sold by many aquatic plant nurseries and garden centres and, while these are effective for a short period of time, they are not a substitute for a properly balanced pool. Some are successful in temporarily clearing the water of fine suspended algae, while others will kill blanketweed and silkweed. In the latter case it is important to remove the dead algae as this will deoxygenate the water during its decomposition and may asphyxiate the fish.

Another kind of cloudiness is caused by the fish stirring up mud and sediment on the floor of the pool. Covering the bottom of the pool and the tops of the planting baskets with a layer of well-washed pea gravel usually prevents this recurring.

Unfortunately, a blue or milky cloudiness is not so easily corrected. This is generally caused by a decomposing body or bodies polluting the water and is usually accompanied by an unpleasant smell. In all but the mildest of cases the pool should be emptied, any accumulated sediment on the bottom removed, and then refilled with fresh water.

Sometimes in country districts a pool will take on a purplish tinge, a curious slimy jelly appears around the perimeter, and the fish and plants start to die. This is invariably the result of a chemical spray having entered the pool, either as spray drift, or on the feet or plumage of wild birds bathing in the margins. While little can be done to control spray drift, by planting the margins thickly with irises and rushes the splashing of birds in the shallows can be eliminated. Once a chemical has entered a pond and caused widespread damage, it is essential to take everything out and scrub the entire pool several times, emptying and refilling with clean water before restocking with fish and plants.

Pests and diseases

Apart from unsavoury occurrences in the water, various pests and diseases manifest themselves on both plants and fish.

Water lily aphids are one of the most frequent assailants

of aquatic plants, particularly water lilies and succulent marginal plants like arrowheads and flowering rush. The aphids smother the entire foliage and secrete a sticky substance over it known as honeydew. This is then prey to a secondary attack by the sooty mould fungus. Widespread disfigurement of both leaves and buds is inevitable, unless the aphids are noticed immediately they take up residence and are washed into the pool with a strong jet of clear water, hopefully to be eaten by the goldfish. Spraying of nearby plum and cherry trees during winter with a tar oil winter wash assists in controlling these pests, as it is in the fissures of bark on the boughs of these trees that the overwintering eggs are deposited.

The black shiny grub of the water lily beetle is another common pest which attacks the foliage of water lilies and pond lilies, almost entirely destroying it. Control by chemical means is impossible where fish are present, so once again a strong jet of clear water is the only safe way of dislodging these pests. Removing the dead and untidy foliage of marginal subjects during the autumn helps considerably in reducing the spread of the beetles by denying them winter protection.

A pond snail that is often introduced into the pool, in the mistaken belief that it will consume algae, causes havoc with water lilies and other succulent-leafed aquatics, chewing ragged lumps out of the leaves which eventually turn yellow and decay. This is the freshwater whelk, a handsome fellow with a pointed spiral shell little more than an inch tall. Once introduced to the pool, it reproduces rapidly and soon constitutes a threat to plant life. Its voracious appetite for succulent foliage is its downfall, for, if a lettuce leaf is floated on the surface of the water, all the snails in the vicinity will congregate beneath and they can then be easily removed and destroyed. New plants that are going to be introduced to the pool should also be inspected for cylinders of clear, jelly-like eggs. These should be removed as they belong to this troublesome pest.

Fortunately, few diseases are specific to aquatic plants, but water lily root rot is not infrequently encountered and is most pernicious, especially on mottled-foliage varieties. The whole crown becomes a horrible smelly mess, and the leaves turn yellow and become detached from the rootstock. Although it is possible to cure plants when caught in the early stages of the disease, it is much more practical to remove and burn diseased crowns and replace with fresh healthy stock.

Unlike plants, fish are subject to a number of diseases. Commonest of these is fish fungus in its various forms. In most cases it appears as a growth like cotton wool clinging to the gills, eyes and mouth, and invading any area of the body that has been damaged. Curing mildly or moderately afflicted fish is relatively easy by the use of fungus cures based upon malachite green or methylene blue. This also applies to the condition known as fin rot in which both tail and fins gradually rot away. But with severe cases of both diseases the kindest way out is to destroy the unfortunate victim.

White spot disease is often encountered with newly purchased fish. Usually its occurrence in the pool can be directly attributed to the introduction of new fish and, if the water is warm, it will rapidly spread to the other inmates. As the speed at which its life cycle is completed is dependent upon the temperature of the water, it is not a problem during early or late season when the water is cool. Fish that are badly infested become covered in myriad small white spots, swim badly and are best destroyed. Mildly affected fish are easily treated with a proprietary white spot cure based upon quinine salts.

Dropsy or scale protrusion is a bacterial disorder which causes the fish to become distended and the scales to stand out from the body. Commercially, this disorder can be cured with antibiotics, but the pool owner's fish are best destroyed before they become too distended.

Sometimes a fish loses its balance and swims upside down or with its nose pointing downwards. This is a physiological disorder generally caused by a deranged swim bladder. There is no certain cure and persistent sufferers should be destroyed. Isolating the fish in water at a stable temperature sometimes alleviates the problem.

Occasionally fish suffer abrasions and lose some scales. When this is noticed it is wise to net the damaged fish and dip it in a methylene blue based fungus cure to restrict the chances of infection.

Dealing with herons

Herons often make themselves a nuisance, even in quite densely populated areas. They spot their prey from the air and, having successfully visited the pool, continue to do so until all the sizeable fish have been taken. Herons generally fish at dawn before the gardener has stirred and it may be some time before the pool-owner is aware that his fish are disappearing. As herons fish while standing in the pool, it is a simple matter to deter them. Erect a small fence around the pool consisting of short canes about 15 cm (6 in) high, linked together with a single strand of fishing line. This will not be visible to the heron, who will touch it with his legs. After several attempts at different points around the pool, he will move on. Herons seem to be incapable of stepping over the deterrent. Netting is sometimes sold to keep herons at bay, but this is difficult to maintain in good order, as plants become entangled in it and look unsightly.

INDEX